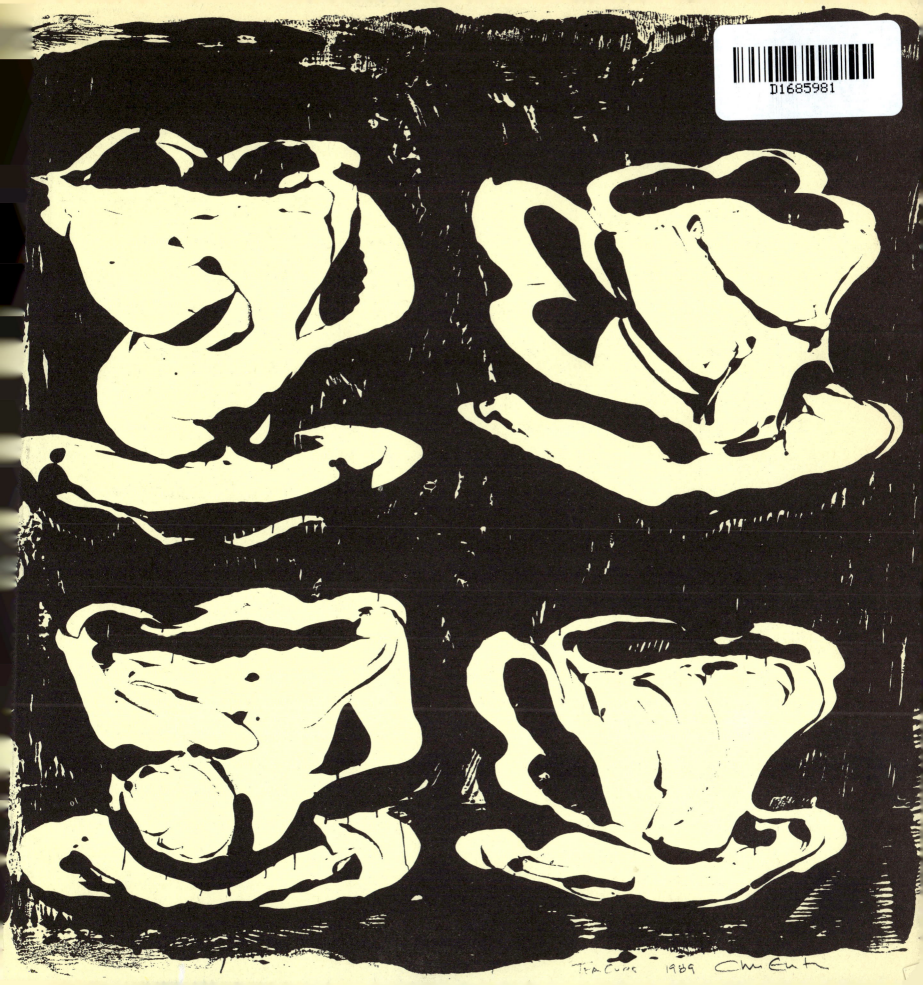

Tea Cups 1989

Tea Cups 1989 Clu Euta

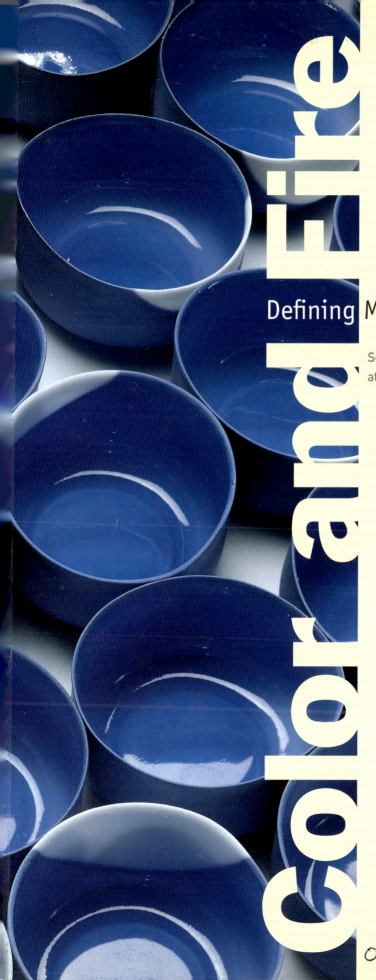

Color and Fire

Defining Moments in Studio Ceramics, 1950–2000

Selections from the Smits Collection and Related Works
at the Los Angeles County Museum of Art

Jo Lauria

with contributions by

Gretchen Adkins

Garth Clark

Rebecca Niederlander

Susan Peterson

Peter Selz

LACMA in association with
Rizzoli International Publications, Inc.

ISBN: 0-8478-2254-0
LC: 99-69987

First published in the United States in 2000 by the Los Angeles
County Museum of Art, 5905 Wilshire Boulevard, Los Angeles,
California 90036, and Rizzoli International Publications, Inc., 300 Park
Avenue South, New York, NY 10010, in conjunction with the exhibition
Color and Fire: Defining Moments in Studio Ceramics, 1950–2000,
organized by the Los Angeles County Museum of Art.

Printed and bound in Italy.
Distributed by St. Martin's Press.

Editor: Margaret Gray
Designer: Katherine Go
Photographer: Steve Oliver
Production manager: Rachel Ware-Zooi

Itinerary of the Exhibition

Los Angeles County Museum of Art
June 4–September 17, 2000

Kemper Museum of Contemporary Art, Kansas City
December 15, 2000–March 4, 2001

The Tucson Museum of Art and Historic Block
April 1–May 30, 2001

Memorial Art Gallery of the University of Rochester
July 29–October 7, 2001

A portion of Garth Clark's essay originally appeared as "Abstract
Expressionism Revisited: The Otis Years, 1954–1959," in *Ceramics: Art
and Perception*, no. 29 (1997): 33–40.

All objects illustrated in color are from the collection of the Los
Angeles County Museum of Art.

Most photographs are reproduced courtesy of the creators or lendors
of the artworks depicted. For certain documentary photographs we have
been unable to trace copyright holders. We would appreciate notification
of same for acknowledgment in future editions.

All sketches and studies are courtesy of the artists.

Front cover:
John Mason, United States, b. 1927.
Red X, 1966. Ceramic. W.: 59½ in. Gift
of the Kleiner Foundation. M.73.38.11.

Endpapers:
Christopher Gustin, United States,
b. 1952. *Teacups,* 1989.

Title page:
Piet Stockmans, Belgium, b. 1940.
Untitled (two views), 1998. Porcelain.
Platter diam.: 18¾ in. Cup h.: ¾ in.
each. Smits Ceramics Purchase Fund.
AC1999.6.1.1–.113.

Back cover:
(Left)
Magdalene Odundo, Kenya, active
England, b. 1950. *Vessel #11,* 1995. Red
earthenware, hand built, burnished,
and reduction fired. H.: 22 in. Smits
Ceramics Purchase Fund. AC1995.90.1.

(Right)
Gertrud Natzler, Austria, active
United States, 1908–1971. **Otto
Natzler,** Austria, active United States,
b. 1908. *Double-Curved Bottle* (*J276*),
1957. Earthenware with cherry-red
glaze. H.: 22 in. Gift of Howard and
Gwen Laurie Smits. M.87.1.103.

Opposite:
Roy Lichtenstein, United States,
1923–1997. *Six-Piece Place Setting,*
1966. Stoneware. Cup h.: 2½ in.
Dinner plate diam.: 10 in. Gift of
Howard and Gwen Laurie Smits.
M.87.1.83, M.87.1.84. © Estate of Roy
Lichtenstein.

Contents

This exhibition attests to the vital, innovative, and deeply imaginative nature of contemporary ceramics over the last fifty years. During this period, the Los Angeles County Museum of Art's permanent collection of ceramic art has grown large and diverse, reflecting the museum's goal of assembling a comprehensive range of work from the postwar years to the millennium. Each sculpture, vessel, and teapot has been selected for its ability to represent the time and place in which it was created. We are proud to be able to offer our public this rich survey of the artistic currents, methods, movements, and formal and intellectual concerns of contemporary ceramics from 1950 to 2000.

LACMA's assistant curator of decorative arts, Jo Lauria, has worked for the past five years to strengthen and expand the collection and to organize this show, a major traveling exhibition of works from this collection. She has written an illuminating introduction for this catalogue that charts the museum's ceramics exhibition and collection history and outlines future goals in this area.

Foreword

LACMA owes all of its great collections to the generosity of its supporters. This exhibition is a tribute to the benefactors whose many gifts have formed the contemporary ceramics collection. Deserving of our most sincere gratitude are the collector Gwen Laurie Smits and her late husband, Howard Smits, whose contributions of more than three hundred contemporary ceramics over the course of the last fifteen years have formed the core of our collection. Their outstanding generosity has also provided for continued acquisitions through the establishment of a purchase fund in their name. Many of the exceptional pieces in this catalogue and exhibition are the result of this benevolence. We applaud such long-standing commitment and inspired vision. We also owe a debt of gratitude to the late Rose A. Sperry, collector of Gertrud and Otto Natzler vessels, and the late Betty M. Asher, collector of contemporary teacups, for the major donations of their entire collections. Further, subsequent individual donations have continued to strengthen this core. We are sincerely grateful to all of our patrons, who have, together, contributed to forming this substantial collection for the community of Los Angeles.

Andrea L. Rich
President and Director
Los Angeles County Museum of Art

Acknowledgments
Jo Lauria

Many people contributed their knowledge and expertise to *Color and Fire: Defining Moments in Studio Ceramics, 1950–2000.* Although it is the responsibility of the curator to develop the scope and specific content of an exhibition and its accompanying catalogue, the ultimate success of the project depends on the cooperative efforts and intellectual energies of all the museum staff and other colleagues who assist in realizing it from inception to completion.

In the beginning, this project benefited from the scholarship of Martha Drexler Lynn, former associate curator of decorative arts and author of LACMA's first catalogue on contemporary ceramics, *Clay Today: Contemporary Ceramists and Their Work* (1990). Lynn laid the foundation on which I have built as I endeavored to relate another chapter of the story of postwar ceramics. I also owe a debt of gratitude to Leslie Bowman, former head of the Department of Decorative Arts, for providing insight as I began to conceptualize the exhibition. This project would not have gone forward without Bowman's support.

Others in the Department of Decorative Arts to whom I am grateful are Martin Chapman, acting head, for taking up the reins and overseeing this project in its final stages, and Maile Pingel, curatorial administrator, who with grace and cheer has been unfailingly helpful in tracking the myriad details of exhibition organization. I would also like to acknowledge the efforts of J. Collin Gleason, curatorial summer intern, who helped compile the bibliography, and Rebecca Niederlander, research assistant par excellence, who responded with unwavering courtesy and resourcefulness. Our department volunteers, Marilyn Gross and Cornelia Bailey, deserve warmest thanks for their tireless efforts and painstaking attention to detail.

Graham Beal, former director of LACMA, and Andrea L. Rich, president and director, supported this project from the start and provided the resources for its development. A hearty thanks also goes to our exhibition programs staff, under the leadership of its assistant director, Irene Martin. Thanks especially to Christine Lazzaretto, exhibition programs coordinator, whose generosity and expert organization of the national tour are much appreciated. I am also thankful to Jane Burrell, head of the Education Department, for her support and wise counsel in guiding the exhibition video, which has been deftly directed and produced by Elvin Whitesides and Megan Melby of the Audiovisual Department. I applaud you all for these efforts.

I would also like to recognize the museum staff involved in the design and installation of the exhibition. Bernard Kester, exhibition designer, brilliantly met the challenge of creating an exceptional visual environment for this large and diverse collection of art. Further, the exhibition could not have been accomplished without the professionalism and patience of the staff of the Registrar's Office, particularly Jennifer Yates, or without the expert planning and resources of the Operations Department, headed by Art Owens and under the direction of Bill Stahl. Also commendable are the extraordinary commitment and conscientiousness of our collections management and art preparation staff, led by Renée Montgomery; Holly Rittenhouse, Mike Tryon, and Jeff Haskin have been especially helpful. The expertise and advice of conservator Maureen Russell was also key to this enterprise.

Other museum staff and colleagues deserve recognition for their contributions to this catalogue. The excellent librarians in LACMA's research library, Deborah Barlow Smedstad, Grant Rusk, Angelo Gabriel, and especially Ann Diederick, were instrumental in helping me to compile the history that is the subject of my introduction. I am indebted to our photographer, Steve Oliver, and the head of Photographic Services, Peter Brenner, for their uncompromising technical skills and sensitivity to the objects, which are in all instances photographed beautifully. Margaret Gray, the editor of this catalogue, provided invaluable assistance in clarifying the essays, and gentle but expert ministrations in organizing the book. Thanks also to Garrett White, director of publications, for his role in producing this catalogue. Acknowledgment and gratitude are also extended to Linda Sunshine, independent consultant, and Marta Hallett, publisher of Rizzoli, for having the vision to take on this project, and for their expert professional efforts in guiding it to press. The catalogue's handsome and innovative design is the work of Katherine Go, with assistance from Paul Wehby. Because of their talents, long after the exhibition closes, the ideas and images presented in this volume will have an enduring life.

I offer thanks and admiration to the guest authors, Gretchen Adkins, Garth Clark, Rebecca Niederlander, Susan Peterson, and Peter Selz, who have made significant contributions to the literature with their enlightening essays. I am also appreciative of the Herculean efforts of Kathleen Garfield, Sam Jornlin, Susan Peterson, and Pauline Blank in locating and supplying archival photographs. To our rights and reproductions staff, Cheryle Robertson and Shaula Coyl, who graciously rose to the daunting challenge of researching these photographs, I am also grateful.

Many friends and colleagues provided stimulating and enriching discussions about the critical issues of contemporary ceramics, helping to clarify the direction of this exhibition and catalogue. I thank you—Wayne Kuwada, Lois Boardman, Frank Lloyd, Ralph Bacerra, Bernard Kester, Phyllis Green, Gretchen Adkins, and Adrian Saxe—for your honest and critical artistic guidance; you have all proved to be beneficent and wise counselors. Heartfelt thanks are due also to my family, Michael, Alex, and Mackenzie, for their support and cheerfulness throughout the long process of readying an exhibition and a book.

Financial assistance for this catalogue has come from the Andrew W. Mellon Curatorial Support Endowment. This foundation underwrote research travel with a grant, as part of its ongoing program to support scholarship within the museum community. We acknowledge also the great generosity of the Pasadena Art Alliance and the Hillcrest Foundation for their recent grants to underwrite the educational programs associated with this exhibition. Likewise, the organization Friends of Contemporary Ceramics committed funds toward educational needs. These subsidies will enhance our educational programs and ultimately enable our viewers to have a better understanding of the field.

Finally, I wish to acknowledge the donors to LACMA's collection, both private collectors and galleries, whose gifts of important contemporary ceramics have become contributions to our country's artistic heritage and visual culture and have made this exhibition possible. Their names are listed on page 10. The gifts of several major donors, including Rose A. Sperry, Betty M. Asher, and Howard and Gwen Laurie Smits, are discussed at length in my introduction. Here, however, I would like to recognize and applaud the most recent donations of Lynn and Jerry Myers, who have made a significant gift this year of many prized pieces from their collection. It is particularly satisfying to know that Lynn Myers began collecting contemporary ceramics after visiting the exhibition *Contemporary Ceramics from the Smits Collection* at LACMA in 1987. It is the hope of Lynn and Jerry Myers that visitors to *Color and Fire* will also be inspired to become passionate collectors.

In closing, and most importantly, our thanks go to the artists, whose works are the wellspring of inspiration for this project. Their legacy, as documented in this exhibition and catalogue, will inspire future generations with a richer understanding of the art of ceramics.

James Makins, United States, b. 1946. *Tray with Four Cups,* c. 1985. Porcelain. Tray w.: 15¼ in. Cup h.: 2¼ in. each. Gift of Howard and Gwen Laurie Smits in honor of LACMA's twenty-fifth anniversary. M.90.82.37a–e.

Donors to LACMA's Collection of Contemporary Ceramics

Major Donors

Howard and Gwen Laurie Smits,
    Smits Ceramics Purchase Fund
Leonard and Rose A. Sperry, Rose
    A. Sperry 1972 Revocable Trust
Betty M. Asher
Michael Asher and Pamela Sue Allen,
    Betty M. Asher Estate
Lynn and Jerry Myers

Individuals

Laura Ackerman
Laura Andreson
Ralph Bacerra
Lisa Bauer and Stephen Dart
Kathy Bao Bean
Pauline Blank
Herbert and Jean Bloch
Lois and Bob Boardman
Karen Johnson Boyd
Rena Bransten
Allan Chasanoff
Donald Clark
Garth Clark and Mark del Vecchio
Anne B. and Marvin H. Cohen
Dr. Jay Cooper
Charles Cowles
Tom Dunaski
Howard Farber
Dan and Jeanne Fauci
Martha Fulton
Marc and Diane Grainer
Jeff Guido
Otto Heino
Coille Hooven
George Hrycun
Harrison Jedel
Sonny and Gloria Kamm

Richard and Margaret Kavesh
Bernard Kester
Hannah and Russ Kully
Frank Lloyd
Dr. David Meltzer
Catherine McIntosh
Jonathan Nelson
Gay B. Odmark
Maureen O'Reilly
Daniel Ostroff
Max Palevsky
Susan Peterson
Sue and Bernie Pucker
Roy Rydell
Linda Leonard Schlenger
Nancy Selvin
Stanley and Betty Sheinbaum
Barbara Shire
Joel and Judith Slutzky
Peter Staley
Lizbeth Stewart
Melinda M. and Paul R. C. Sullivan
Connie Tavel
Laurie and Eric Terhorst
Mr. and Mrs. Paul LeBaron Thiebaud
Ken and Rebecca Wang
Paula Winokur
Robert Winokur
Marvin and Judy Zeidler
Rosalind Turner Zuses

Galleries

Garth Clark Gallery, New York
Corinth Ceramics Studio, Los Angeles
Helen Drutt, Philadelphia
Ferrin Gallery, Northhampton,
    Massachusetts
Barry Friedman, Ltd., New York

Galerie b15, Munich
Gump's San Francisco
Frank Lloyd Gallery, Santa Monica,
    California
John Natsoulas Gallery, Davis,
    California
Max Protetch, New York
Revolution, A Gallery Project,
    Ferndale, Michigan
Shaw Guido Gallery, Farmington Hills,
    Michigan
Holly Solomon Gallery, New York
Sybaris Gallery, Royal Oak, Michigan
Chen Wang Porcelain, San Diego
Dorothy Weiss Gallery, San Francisco

LACMA and Friends

Art Museum Council Fund
Decorative Arts Council
Friends of Clay
Friends of Contemporary Ceramics
Hillcrest Foundation
Kleiner Foundation
Howard Kottler Testamentary Trust
The Harry and Yvonne Lenart Fund
Modern and Contemporary Art
    Council Fund
Modern and Contemporary Art
    Council Purchase Fund
Modern and Contemporary Art
    Council Young Talent Award
Pasadena Art Alliance

Opposite:
Edward Eberle, United States,
b. 1944. *Sentinel,* 1995. Porcelain.
H.: 19 in. Smits Ceramics Purchase
Fund. AC1996.20.1.1–.2.

Mapping the History of a Collection

Defining Moments in Ceramics at LACMA

Color and Fire: Defining Moments in Studio Ceramics, 1950–2000, is the first
major exhibition organized by the Los Angeles County Museum of Art
from its entire permanent collection of contemporary ceramics.
The exhibition surveys the major stylistic movements in
the history of ceramics during the second half of the twentieth century—from pure functionalism, to functional
references and the nonfunctional, to the ultimate privi-
leging of ideas and content over material and craft.
The selected works chronicle significant achieve-
ments from midcentury to the millennium,
documenting the evolving strategies of ceramic
artists and revealing the intersections of this
medium's history with the broader history of
twentieth-century art.

JO LAURIA

    For the purposes of this exhibition, modern
and contemporary ceramics are defined as
unique clay objects created after 1925 by one or
a pair of artists working in a studio environment.
The year 1925 is our departmental demarcation of
the end of the Arts and Crafts era, when most art
pottery was produced in a factory setting by teams
of skilled artisans who specialized in the separate
functions of shaping, decorating, glazing, and firing.
A contemporary studio ceramist, by contrast, is the sole
creator of a piece, from its initial concept through every stage
of its aesthetic development.

Opposite, left:
John Mason, United States,
b. 1927. *Spear Form,* 1963.
Stoneware. H.: 59½ in. Smits
Ceramics Purchase Fund.
AC1997.38.1.

Opposite, right:
Peter Voulkos, United
States, b. 1924. *5000 Feet,* 1958.
Ceramic. H.: 45½ in. Purchase
Award, Artists of Los Angeles
and Vicinity Annual Exhibition,
LACMA, 1959. M.59.16.

Gertrud Natzler, Austria, active
United States; 1908–1971. **Otto
Natzler,** Austria, active United
States, b. 1908. *Teardrop Bottle
(L385),* 1961. Earthenware with
gray celadon reduction glaze
with melt fissures and carbon
deposits. H.: 9⁷⁄₁₆ in. Gift of Rose
A. Sperry 1972 Revocable Trust.
M.72.105.44.

LACMA's long-standing commitment to acquiring and exhibiting contemporary ceramics has resulted in a collection acknowledged for its depth, diversity, and quality. It includes a wide historical range of both traditional vessel forms and large-scale sculptures from the United States, Europe, Scandinavia, Australia, Asia, and Mexico, with a major concentration in U.S. and British studio pottery. The collection's particular richness is evident in its holdings of works by the renowned California artists Robert Arneson, Ralph Bacerra, Viola Frey, Glen Lukens, John Mason, Harrison McIntosh, Ken Price, Adrian Saxe, and Peter Voulkos. It also contains the most extensive representation in any public institution of vessels by the internationally acclaimed artists Gertrud and Otto Natzler. Although the collection and exhibition include work from the 1930s and 1940s, the primary focus is ceramic art produced between 1950 and the present.

The history of the discipline during this period can be seen as a series of "defining moments"—shifts in direction, perception, or philosophy due to the fateful convergence of artists and thinkers. Both centers of energy and catalysts of change, defining moments activate, agitate, expand, promote, and transcend art-making. Each is a flash point that burns red hot and ignites fires of creativity, short lived but with a lasting impact on artists and art movements.

These defining historical moments have frequently corresponded to significant points in LACMA's history, as the museum has been actively involved in exhibiting and collecting contemporary ceramics from the outset of the movement. The story of LACMA's collection is therefore, to some degree, connected with the story of ceramics over the past fifty years. This essay charts the points where these histories have converged.

Building a Collection, Realizing a Mission

In postwar exhibition history, the first LACMA-organized venue in which artists had the opportunity to exhibit ceramic sculpture was *Artists of Los Angeles and Vicinity,* an annual exhibition at the museum's former location in Exposition Park, Los Angeles. (LACMA moved to its current location in 1965.) Between 1940 and 1961, these juried shows exhibited paintings, drawings and prints, and sculptures. One of the earliest inclusions by a ceramic artist, in 1957, was a sculptural vessel by Peter Voulkos (b. 1924) entitled *Walking Woman.*[1] Voulkos is the leading figure in postwar ceramics, and his impact continues to shape the field. But at

Catalogue cover for the exhibition *Artists of Los Angeles and Vicinity,* LACMA, 1957. Peter Voulkos, among other significant Los Angeles artists of the 1950s, exhibited his sculptures and paintings in these annual juried shows.

that time he was a relatively young artist who in 1954 had been appointed chairman of the Ceramics Department at Otis Art Institute. (This school's official name at the time was the Los Angeles County Art Institute, but it was referred to as Otis, after the family name of its original benefactor. Today it is the Otis College of Art and Design.) Voulkos had also garnered attention through his first one-person exhibition at Felix Landau Gallery in Los Angeles (April 1956). According to a reviewer, Voulkos's exhibition revealed "the new approach of form and decoration that he has taken in the last year.... A number of pieces were boldly asymmetrical. There were multiform vases four feet high in which wheel-thrown elements of varying size and shape had been joined together."[2] This quality of asymmetrical assemblage also characterizes *Walking Woman* and the more overtly sculptural pieces Voulkos submitted to the *Artists of Los Angeles and Vicinity* annuals in 1958 and 1959.[3]

In 1958 Voulkos offered for competition an almost three-foot-tall, monochromatic, black-stained clay sculpture of stacked, closed vessel-like forms, *Burnt Smog* (p. 16). In the 1959 annual he submitted a second piece from this series,[4] his celebrated sculpture *5000 Feet,* 1958 (p. 12), which won a Purchase as well as a Prize Award (from juror New York sculptor David Smith) and thus become part of LACMA's permanent collection. *5000 Feet* marks a significant transition: Voulkos had transformed his sculptural wheel-thrown and altered pots—such as *Standing Jar,* 1954–56 (p. 121), which is still defined by the base, belly, shoulder, and opened lip of a pot—into massive, purely sculptural structures now liberated from imposed vessel constraints.

In the catalogue for Voulkos's second one-man show at Felix Landau Gallery, in 1959, Dr. Thomas W. Leavitt, director of the Pasadena

Peter Voulkos, United States, b. 1924. *Gallas Rock,* 1961. Clay, fired. H.: 84 in. This sculpture, from the collection of Mr. and Mrs. Digby Gallas, was one of the works in clay and bronze exhibited in Voulkos's solo exhibition, *Sculpture,* held on the plaza at LACMA in 1965.

Peter Voulkos, United States, b. 1924. *Burnt Smog* (also known as *Burned Smog* and *Funiculation Smog*) c. 1957. Ceramic. H.: approx. 35 in. Photograph courtesy of Peter Voulkos. Voulkos entered this sculpture in the 1958 *Artists of Los Angeles and Vicinity* juried show at LACMA. It is now in the collection of Fallingwater, the house designed by Frank Lloyd Wright for Edgar J. Kaufmann in Bear Run, Pennsylvania.

Fritz Wotruba, Austria, 1907–1975. *Figural Composition,* 1951. Stone. H.: 20 in. Photograph © F. Radax. Wotruba's work, exhibited in a touring show at LACMA in 1955, may have inspired Voulkos to build monumental clay sculptures by anchoring multiple elements to a central axis.

Peter Voulkos in his studio on Glendale Boulevard, Los Angeles, with one of his large ceramic sculptures (later destroyed), c. 1959. Photograph by John Mason, courtesy of Peter Voulkos.

Art Museum, praised Voulkos as a pioneer of "new ideas of basic significance": "In 1958, he added an altogether new dimension to his work, creating large, free-standing ceramic sculpture. Over a clay skeleton, he applies forms originally thrown on a wheel and then cut and modeled to desired shapes. When the sculpture is completely formed, glaze is applied and the piece is placed in a giant kiln. Firing problems are acute because the forms are complicated and the scale is often monumental. His success in this medium could prove to be a major achievement in twentieth-century sculpture."[5]

Voulkos's technical innovations in clay may have been unprecedented, but he had been inspired to create his towering works of stacked and cantilevered components by the stone-carved and bronze figurative sculptures of Austrian artist Fritz Wotruba, which he had seen at an exhibition at LACMA (September 4 to October 2, 1955). Wotruba's canted and finely balanced volumetric sculptures deeply influenced Voulkos, suggesting to him a method of achieving mass and vertical thrust by anchoring an assemblage of piled elements to a central axis.[6] LACMA later played a role in exhibiting and collecting Voulkos's monumental ceramic sculpture, which represents one of the most significant artistic breakthroughs and defining moments in the field.

Peter Voulkos working on a stack form, 1993.
Photograph © 1993 Sam Jornlin, courtesy
of Peter Voulkos.

Peter Voulkos, United States,
b. 1924. *Big Missoula*, 1995.
Stoneware, wood fired. H.: 41 in.
Smits Ceramics Purchase Fund.
AC1996.61.1

Peter Voulkos, United States. *Untitled,* 1996. Drypoint. Image: 12 x 9 in. Sheet: 20 x 15 in. Chopmark: MA Nose Studios, Robert Brinker, printer. Collection of Sam Jornlin. Photograph courtesy of Peter Voulkos.

Giving Rein to Abstract Expressionism

In the *Artists of Los Angeles and Vicinity* annual exhibitions of 1957 to 1961 (the last year the annual was held), several pivotal works in the Abstract Expressionist style were entered by Michael Frimkess (b. 1937), John Mason (b. 1927), Jerry Rothman (b. 1933), and Henry Takemoto (b. 1933). These artists were students of Voulkos, who, along with Billy Al Bengston (b. 1934), Mac McClain (b. 1923), Ken Price (b. 1935), and Paul Soldner (b. 1921), participated in the vibrant pot shop at the Otis Art Institute.[7] Together they radicalized traditional approaches to clay and changed the direction of ceramics with their abstract, nonobjective, improvisational sculpture.

Rose Slivka, editor of *Craft Horizons,* used this work as the basis for her landmark 1961 article "The New Ceramic Presence." The creation of ceramic sculpture, she announced, had become a legitimate aesthetic pursuit, rising out of, and taking its cue from, the Abstract Expressionist painting movement: "So great a catalyst has been American painting that the odyssey from surface to form has been made through its power. Manipulating form as far as it could go to project the excitement of surface values, the potters found even the slightest concession of function too limiting." Slivka perceived that this new attitude had also affected traditional potters:

"The developments in abstract sculpture have decidedly affected the formal environment of ceramists everywhere. The decision of the sculptor to reinterpret the figure as well as all organic form through abstraction and even to project intellectually devised forms with no objective reference inevitably enlarged the formal vistas of every craftsman and designer working in three dimensions.

To pottery, sculpture has communicated its own sense of release from the tyranny of traditional tools and materials, a search for new ways of treating materials and for new forms to express new images and new ideas."[8]

Although Slivka did not name the new approach, she gave credence to the concept of a style in ceramics that shared the spirit and approach of Abstract Expressionist painting: "The sculptor today places greater emphasis on event rather than occasion, in the force of movement and the stance of the dance rather than in the power of permanence and the weight of immobility, in the metamorphosis of meanings rather than in the eternity of symbols."[9] Here she was following the path freshly cleared by the critic Harold Rosenberg, who in 1952 had identified and celebrated a "new presence" in painting: "The canvas began to appear to one American painter after another as an arena in which to act—rather than as a space in which to reproduce, redesign, analyze, or 'express' an object, actual or imagined. What was to go on the canvas was not a picture but an event."[10]

The new ceramic presence became further entrenched in the mid-1960s, when LACMA organized solo shows for both Voulkos and Mason, the critically recognized front-runners working in the Abstract Expressionist style. Voulkos's exhibition, curated by Maurice Tuchman and titled simply *Sculpture* (April 14 to June 20, 1965), was a presentation on the museum's plaza of four monumental, characteristically craggy and muscular ceramic sculptures and six large-scale sculptures of cast bronze with aluminum and steel. (Voulkos had begun to work in bronze and other metals in 1960, after moving north to teach at the University of California at Berkeley in 1959.) The critic Nancy Marmer cited the massive, seven-foot-high clay sculpture *Gallas Rock,* 1961 (p. 15), as an example of Voulkos's deeper exploration of the relationship of sculptural form to surface treatment: "Again Voulkos builds up a tightly coherent form from separate bulky masses, but here the pallid, unglazed clay has torn edges, dark declivities, opened out hollows, and cryptic inner spaces which accentuate contrasts of light and shadow. The relationship of part to part is often unexpected and adds an excited rhythm to the work."[11] These attributes resurface with assertiveness and refinement in Voulkos's later work, particularly his gestural plates and stacks with their rips, punctures, and dramatic rhythmic lines. His characteristic imprints are clearly developed in later work such as *Large Plate,* 1979 (p. 150) and *Big Missoula,* 1995 (p. 18).

John Mason's one-person exhibition at LACMA the next year (November 16, 1966 to February 1, 1967) was also curated by Maurice Tuchman and had the same economical title as Voulkos's—*Sculpture.* Like Voulkos, Mason had already established a name for himself through major gallery exhibitions. He had exhibited at the Ferus Gallery in Los Angeles since 1957, with favorably reviewed solo shows in 1958, 1959, and 1961. His LACMA exhibition was also installed on the museum's plaza, which proved just large enough to contain sixteen grandly scaled sculptures. Included were representative pieces from five distinct series Mason had executed between 1963 and 1966: buoyantly expressionistic totemic spear forms, from five to nine feet tall; vigorously manipulated crosslike forms; monumental walls modeled in deep relief; monoliths; and geometric forms in bright colors. In the catalogue, John Coplans emphasized

View of the exhibition *John Mason: Sculpture* on the plaza at LACMA, 1966. The show included pieces from five separate series Mason had been working on since 1963: spear forms, crosslike forms, monumental walls, monoliths, and geometric forms.

Opposite:
John Mason, United States, b. 1927. *Red X,* 1966. Ceramic. W.: 59½ in. Gift of the Kleiner Foundation. M.73.38.11.

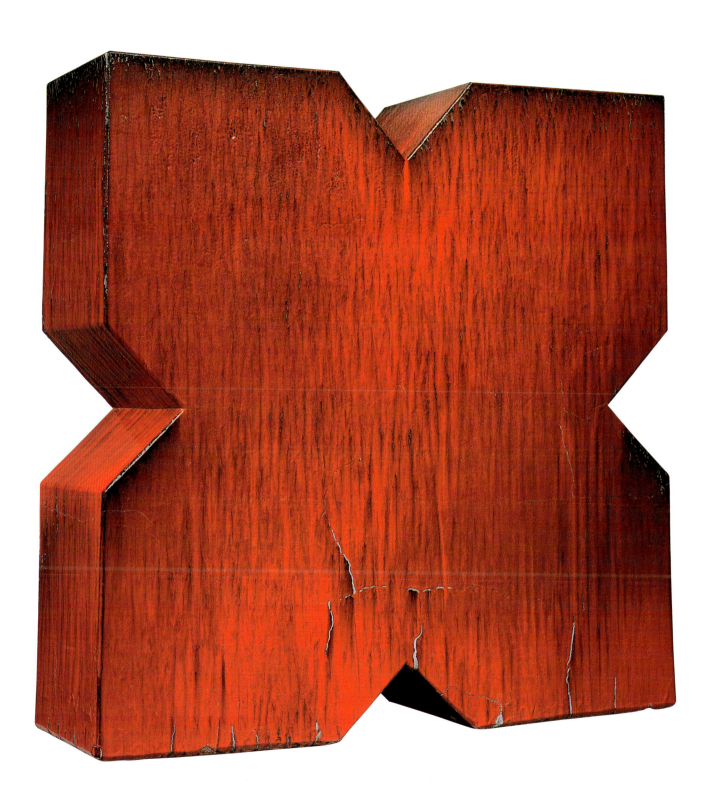

Mason's groundbreaking exploration of clay: "That there has been little or no precedent for the use of this material as a prime medium for ambitious art is now no longer a matter of consequence or any barrier to its usage and acceptance.... The richness and variety of the work Mason has produced over the past decade stand as a testament to the constant and extended dialogue between his artistic aspirations and his means."[12]

Coplans had written incisive articles about the new work in ceramics as early as 1963 for *Artforum* and *Art in America,* directing national attention to this previously uncharted terrain and gaining recognition for ceramics as a vital art discipline.[13] In October 1966, one month before the opening of the Mason exhibition, he had organized *Abstract Expressionist Ceramics* (University of California, Irvine, October 28 to November 27; San Francisco Museum of Art, January 11 to February 12, 1967). This exhibition, which officially named the movement, is now acknowledged as a milestone, as it proclaimed an identifiable and distinctly American attitude in ceramics, "germinal elements" of a style not derivative of a European tradition.[14] Coplans explained that he had selected artists for the exhibition (Billy Al Bengston, Michael Frimkess, John Mason, Mac McClain, James Melchert, Ron Nagle, Manuel Neri, Kenneth Price, Henry Takemoto, and Peter Voulkos) who sensed "the form-expressed emotion that lay at the heart of Abstract Expressionism" and exploited "shape and surface for its expressive potential."[15] (A reevaluation of the Abstract Expressionist ceramics movement is provided in the essay by Garth Clark herein, p. 123.)

John Mason in his studio on Glendale Boulevard in Los Angeles, with work in progress. Vertical sculptures, strip sculptures, and *Grey Wall* behind him, 1960. Photograph courtesy of John Mason.

Mason's exhibition received national coverage.[16] Decades later, these pieces are enjoying a renewed appreciation, which seems to support the claims of those critics who thought the work visionary and ahead of its time. LACMA acquired two Mason sculptures from this period, *Red X,* 1966 (p. 21), and *Spear Form,* 1963 (p. 12). Mason considers *Red X* the most important of the monoliths included in his LACMA show.[17] The art critic Helen Giambruni also singled it out in a review: "The great red X, the center of the show and its best work, is simply inescapable."[18] It remains as vital and evocative today as it was then, with its universal, timeless form, the vivid tension between its hard-edged geometry and its fluid red glaze, and its bold scale, which places it in the realm of the mythical and votive. *Red X* appeared in another LACMA exhibition, *American Sculpture of the Sixties,* in 1967, also curated by Maurice Tuchman.

Spear Form, purchased for the collection in 1997, is of equal importance as a prime example of Mason's early Abstract Expressionist phase. What distinguishes this sculpture as supremely expressionistic is the twisting and torquing of the clay into an asymmetrical tower of manipulated surfaces, which record the artist's touch throughout the creative process. As Mason recalls, "It was very much about the material and the processes that were evident from the form after it was finished.... What its history was, was revealed. And initially it was about process, which in some ways did parallel the abstract expressionists."[19]

The 1960s would prove to be one of the most fertile decades for contemporary ceramics at LACMA. The museum would organize two exhibitions in the summer of 1966: *The Ceramic Work of Gertrud and Otto Natzler* (June 15 to August 14) and *Robert Irwin/Kenneth Price* (July 7 to September 4), and LACMA would receive its first major gift of contemporary ceramics, fifty-four Natzler vessels bequeathed by Rose A. Sperry, in 1968. These events would have lasting impact on the direction of the collection.

An Evolving Relationship between Artist and Museum: The Natzlers and LACMA

The Ceramic Work of Gertrud and Otto Natzler, 1966, was the first full-scale museum retrospective in the United States to be organized for the Natzlers since their arrival in 1938 as Viennese émigrés. With the threat of Nazi persecution—on 11 March 1938 Hitler's forces marched into Vienna and two days later annexed Austria—Gertrud and Otto fled their homeland, boarding an Italian freighter in Trieste. They arrived in Los Angeles in October 1938, bringing an expansive knowledge of ceramic studio production, a refined aesthetic, and an international reputation: Their works had been exhibited at Vienna's Galerie Wurthle in 1937, and they had won the coveted silver medal from the *Exposition Internationale,* Paris, in 1938. When their belongings—a potter's wheel, a small electric kiln, glaze materials, and "one hundred of their best works"—arrived in 1939 by cargo ship, they set up a studio in Los Angeles.[20] They worked as industriously and fluently as an artist team as they had in Vienna, Gertrud sure-handed at the wheel and throwing graceful forms for Otto's inventive glazes.

Gertrud and Otto Natzler at work during an artist residency at Brandeis Camp Institute, c. 1950s. Photograph © Lotte Nossaman, courtesy of Otto and Gail Natzler.

Gertrud Natzler, Austria, active United States; 1908–1971. **Otto Natzler,** Austria, active United States, b. 1908.

Left:
Cylindrical Vase with Indented Lip (M870), 1963. Earthenware with "Nocturne" glaze and deep-olive-to-magenta reduction glaze with melt fissures and crystals. H.: 8⅞ in. Gift of Rose A. Sperry 1972 Revocable Trust. M.72.105.50.

Below:
Bowl (D465), 1952. Earthenware with pale yellow glaze. Diam.: 8¼ in. Gift of Rose A. Sperry 1972 Revocable Trust. M.72.105.25.

Otto Natzler, Austria, active United States, b. 1908. *Green Lichen Cube (X280),* 1982. Earthenware with yellow, gray, and green crater glaze. H.: 12 in. Gift of Howard and Gwen Laurie Smits. M.87.1.109.

From the very beginning of their career in the United States, the Natzlers were engaged with LACMA. They were represented in museum exhibitions from 1939 to 1943 and given a "one-family show" in 1944.[21] Their retrospective in 1966 featured 175 works—bowls, vases, plates, and bottle forms—borrowed from local and national collections. Otto wrote an insightful preface for the catalogue, in which he discussed what he perceived as the undervaluation of their discipline and pronounced their aesthetic philosophy:

"The field we work in is ancient, yet little explored. It is hardly recognized by the public in general who do not associate pots made of ordinary clay with art, unless they happen to be old or decorated. Yet, the objects we make are pots, they are made of clay, they are made today and they are not decorated. Their possible function as containers is unimportant to us.... We believe in evolution, in an aesthetic expression of our thoughts in an expressive medium. We believe in using our fantasy, inspiration, emotions and dreams, but also in restraint when translating them into our work. The really perfect pot has not yet been made and probably never will be. Yet we reach for perfection, and, if we are fortunate, the next pot we make may come closer to our visions."[22]

In this pursuit of perfection, during a thirty-seven-year collaboration, Gertrud formed 25,000 pots, and Otto graced each with one of the 2,500 glazes he developed. Gertrud died of cancer in 1971. After glazing the pots she had left unfinished, Otto forged his own creative path, creating slab-constructed, architectural sculptures, their small scale and vigorously glazed surfaces offsetting their massive weight, acute planes, and solid physicality, as in *Green Lichen Cube (X280),* 1982 (opposite).

From the outset, Natzler vessels were acknowledged as treasures and actively sought by collectors. The art critic Rose Henderson discussed this phenomenon in 1957: "A number of art collectors buy some of the best pots simply as ceramics *per se,* without thinking of their functional use other than the function of art. These collectors are willing to wait months for the production of a pot which the potters consider exceptional."[23] Given the demand and the limited supply of such exceptional pots, it is extraordinary that Leonard and Rose A. Sperry were able to assemble an unparalleled historical collection of pots from 1944 to 1966, which Rose bequeathed to LACMA in 1968.

The Sperrys had met the Natzlers in 1952 and had become their most dedicated collectors, setting out to acquire at least one exemplary pot from each year the Natzlers had worked in this country. On the occasion of the gift, in 1968, LACMA published a catalogue. In her preface, Rose A. Sperry wrote, "I knew that I wanted to have a retrospective collection of Natzler ceramics dating from the first years of their work in the United States. As I thought this through, it became clear to me that one day I should present this collection *in toto* to a leading museum in order that many more people than my intimate group of friends could enjoy it."[24]

LACMA was then and still is the only institution with such an exceptional holding of Natzler pieces. This important gift takes on even greater significance, because it has served as the base upon which LACMA's comprehensive collection of contemporary ceramics has been built.

Moving toward a New Aesthetic

The Natzler retrospective was wholly dissimilar, in its conceptual orientation and content, from *Robert Irwin/ Kenneth Price,* also at LACMA in 1966 (July 7 to September 4). Whereas the Natzlers' classic, domestically scaled vessels personified the perfection of form, profile, and proportion and virtuosity of surface treatment (purist pottery concerns), Price's work represented a distant point on the spectrum. His intimate, abstracted, hot-rod-colored biomorphic shapes (eggs, mounds, undefined tumescent globules, which he called "slurps")[25] and his boxed constructions containing curious "specimens" were sculptural and cerebral and dealt formally with complex contemporary art issues. These stark differences underscore the expanded possibilities available to the artist working with ceramic materials in the late 1960s.

The pairing of Price's ceramic sculptures with Irwin's paintings immediately aligned the works on the same hierarchical plane of fine art, raising ceramics above the minor arts to which the discipline had previously been consigned. Voulkos and Mason had also reached this zenith in the same decade. Their means of ascension was through the production of work that purposely invalidated the principle of function (thereby eliminating the "craft" stigma), redefined the ceramic object's function as wholly aesthetic, and distanced itself from domestic references through monumental scale and mass.

Price had arrived at this plateau on his own terms. In his groundbreaking one-man shows at Ferus Gallery,[26] he exhibited painstakingly fashioned, delicately scaled, ambiguously shaped ovoid sculptures emblazoned with acid colors. Unlike the work of Voulkos and Mason, these objects made no attempt to achieve monumentality and ignored the taboo against ostentatious surface coloration. Price's use of bold, flashy color as fundamental to the form was an approach no one had tried before. He later commented, "They were painted sculptures, and they didn't have any reference to pottery, so I don't think anybody thought about my forms as having anything to do with clay. Painted sculpture was very rare. I felt [John] Chamberlain and I were the only two guys at the time making colored sculpture and dealing with color as an integral part of the form, and not as an afterthought."[27]

Price moved freely from paint to glaze, having been trained as both painter and ceramist. He had studied painting and ceramics formally at the Chouinard Art Institute (1953–54) and at the University of Southern California (BFA, 1956) and worked informally alongside Voulkos at the Otis clay studio (1957–58). In a quest for technical expertise, he attended the New York State College of Ceramics at Alfred University in New York, receiving his MFA in 1959.

Price then moved back to California and had his first one-man show in 1960 at Ferus Gallery, followed by others in 1961 and 1964. As art critic Joan Simon has noted, Price's deep involvement with the Ferus artists decisively influenced his work: "Part of the generation of artists which put the L.A. art scene on the international map in the 1960s, Price... shared with Bengston and Kauffman concerns of craftsmanship, finish and color; with Ruscha, wit and a playful interest in small scale and vernacular types; and (more recently) with Kienholz and Irwin, certain environmental concerns."[28]

View of the *Robert Irwin/Kenneth Price* exhibition at LACMA, 1966.

Cover of the LACMA catalogue for the exhibition *Late Fifties at the Ferus*, 1968, featuring a collage of snapshots of artists associated with the Ferus Gallery.

Announcement for a solo show by Kenneth Price at Ferus Gallery, Los Angeles, 1961. Photograph courtesy of Kenneth Price.

John Coplans was probably the first critic to perceive that the Ferus artists, in particular Craig Kauffman, Robert Irwin, Ken Price, and Billy Al Bengston, shared certain exploratory innovations. In 1964 he wrote, "What these artists have developed is an aggressive and high-spirited arrogance that only young and talented men can have. It is a frontier sensibility—anything a man can stake out for himself is his own; he doesn't have to wait to inherit."[29] Coplans praised these artists for their "venturesomeness" in employing new craft techniques or creating sculptural forms that "break with sacrosanct traditions." He added, "Price is also completely uninhibited by any tradition of technique, form or style.... He will juxtapose the most weird of primordial forms with the most brilliant of colors to create a strange interplay between the joyful and the ominous."[30]

This menacing quality was also noted by Kurt Von Meier, who in a review of the LACMA exhibition proclaimed Price's pieces "prime examples of the aesthetic of nastiness" and "mean-beautiful things."[31] Price employed this seduction/repulsion dialectic by creating candy-colored, slick objects that send forth a come-hither call, only to repel with their wicked open orifices with protruding writhing tendrils or extruded lumpy shapes that recall coiled excrement. This push-pull tension is most dramatically evident in the Specimens, enigmatic clay blobs resting on beds of sand or cushioned pillows and boxed and numbered, which demand to be examined as delicious abnormalities. They powerfully exude the "aura" described by the German philosopher and art historian Walter Benjamin in the 1930s, the capacity of certain objects to transform the surrounding space into one of tantalizing mystery that compels the viewer to come closer to the spectacle, to linger longer, to breathe in and become part of the aura.[32] This phenomenon is also aptly described in the "Rubberneck Manifesto" by Price's contemporary, vanguard artist Robert Williams: "The purest form of art is to give way to simple visual interest. To look at what you find yourself driven to see... when all predetermined prejudices are momentarily set aside and you are one of the many at the scene of the horrible accident your libido will do the looking."[33] Price exploits this effect to the fullest extent by fashioning objects that cause visual and visceral stimulation to take precedence over rationalism. His *Echo,* 1997 (p. 28), the most recent addition to the collection, is a wonderfully mysterious and majestic oversize amoeba form saturated with intoxicatingly bright yellow-gold acrylic paint.

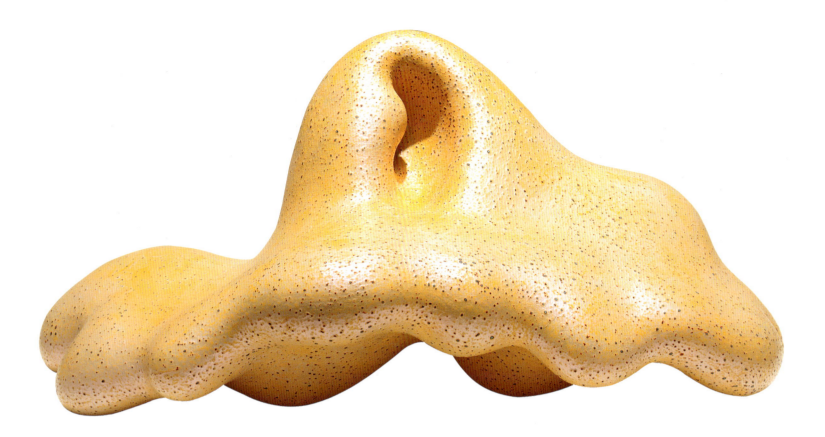

Kenneth Price, United States, b. 1935. *Echo,* 1997. Clay, fired and painted. W.: 26½ in. Purchased with funds provided by Friends of Clay, the Decorative Arts Council, and the Modern and Contemporary Art Department. TR.12786. Photograph by Robert Wedermeyer, courtesy of L.A. Louver Gallery, Venice, California.

Lucy Lippard, in the exhibition catalogue for the Price/Irwin show, had difficulty wedging Price into a canonical category, calling him "something of a Surrealist, something of a purist, something of an expressionist, something of a naturalist." She finally crowned him with "original," the highest modernist accolade: "It is a fact rather than a value judgment that no one else, on the East or West coast, is working like Kenneth Price. He is involved in a peculiarly contemporary dialectic.... His pace, like his morphology, is his own."[34]

In the following decade Price again defined the cutting edge of ceramics with his vanguard installation *Ken Price: Happy's Curios* at LACMA (April 4 to July 2, 1978). The installation included a variety of displays on related themes: ten curio cabinets that Price called "units" or "town units," each stocked with faux-bordertown souvenir ceramics evoking Mexican, Aztec, and Native American traditions; three "death shrines," altars holding cups, bowls, and vases emblazoned with skull imagery (evoking a Mexican Day of the Dead presentation); showcase windows displaying domestic ware decorated with Southwestern folk-culture motifs; and acrylic paintings on paper and colorful wall hangings.

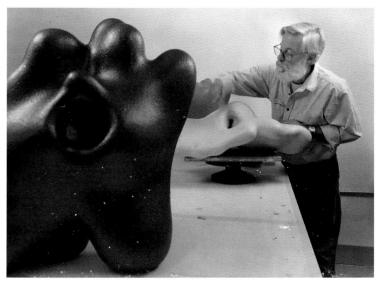

Ken Price in his studio in Taos, New Mexico, working on *Echo*,
1997. Photograph © Paul O'Connor, courtesy of Ken Price.

Price described the installation as a work of "pottery about pottery,"[35] on the one hand paying homage to the authentic but anonymous Mexican and American Indian folk potters who produced low-art wares; on the other commenting on what curator Maurice Tuchman described as the "poor state, and low status, of pottery in the art worlds of the U.S. and Europe."[36] Tuchman framed Price's exacting tableaux as an act of visual ventriloquism: "*Happy's Curios* began with an intense and disciplined effort of psychological projection: Price identified himself with the folk artists who make roadside monuments and the artisans who produce pottery in over 200 villages throughout Mexico.... He determined above all to make a body of work true in spirit to the folk/cottage industry sensibility, that 'easy, off-hand but utterly assured characteristic' of 'low art' pottery."[37]

Price had created all of the components during five years in his studio in Taos, New Mexico, where he had moved in 1971 with his wife, Happy. His original plan was to present the installation as an actual store, "a walk-in sculpture made out of pottery," where "all the pieces were going to be shown together, built into a store, essentially all one 'cabinet' in a building" resulting in "a bombardment of images and color.... Really intense and baroque." But Price discovered "that to do it the way I wanted I was going to have to buy a store. Obviously I couldn't do that."[38] So he altered his plans to fit a gallery setting and designed an exact, controlled, sculptural environment of units that interacted thematically.

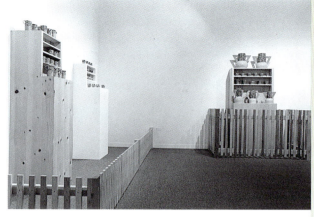

Top:
View of *Ken Price: Happy's Curios* at LACMA, 1978.

Above:
Diagram showing Price's exhibition design for *Happy's Curios.*

Right:
Kenneth Price, United States, b. 1935. *Happy's Curios, Unit 3,* 1972–77. Ceramic with wood cabinet. Cabinet h.: 70 in. Cup h.: 2½ in. each. Gift of Betty M. Asher. M.83.229.25a–r.

Happy's Curios was critically heralded as "one of the major exhibitions of the decade and a challenge to conventional categories of "art" and "craft."[39] Peter Schjeldahl commented on Price's agility in consorting with, and contesting, the shifting line between the major and the minor arts: "*Happy's Curios* drops hints for a shake-up of traditions in sophisticated craft, much as some recent work in painting and sculpture has suggested at least a yearning for a new, late-twentieth century movement in the decorative arts. I don't know what Price thinks he's doing, but I can imagine no more wholesome role for him than, having sneaked his pottery into the museum as art, winning a place for it there as craft. Such a general development seems called for both by the miasmic confusions of contemporary art and by the late-modern mediocrity that clutters up our kitchens and our daily lives."[40]

Components of the original installation at LACMA became highly visible the following year, 1979, when they were selected for both the prestigious Whitney Biennial, New York, and the *Directions* exhibition at the Hirshhorn Museum and Sculpture Garden, Washington, D.C. Two town units, *Unit 2* and *Indian Unit,* also appeared in *West Coast Ceramics,* organized by the Stedelijk Museum, Amsterdam. Rose Slivka, author of the catalogue, describes the work as a miraculous creative feat that engaged the political, cultural, social, and religious spheres of art making: "In the arrangement of what would be, ordinarily, bad taste objects in a shrine-like setting, [Price] imbues them with a mysterious religious power whereby they become high art within the traditional intention of the church which originally separated high and low art.... Although he thinks this is the ultimate in high jinks, it is nothing short of a miracle—the highest purpose of art and, after all, the hope of religion."[41]

Eventually, the units and death shrines of *Happy's Curios* were sold as individual objets d'art. LACMA acquired one of the outstanding cabinets, *Unit 3* (opposite), as part of a major acquisition of cups and cup sculptures from the collection of Betty M. Asher, who had served as assistant curator for *Happy's Curios.*

Asher, who died in 1994 at the age of 80, was legendary for her collection of cups. As artist Adrian Saxe has commented, she "empowered a generation of Californian potters to deal with the vessel as art format. She acknowledged that making a pot, even one as seemingly simple as a cup, was a serious enterprise."[42] Asher began collecting contemporary art in the early 1960s, when she was "the first collector to purchase a work by Andy

Los Angeles collector and dealer Betty M. Asher at home with some of her cups, 1991. *Angeles* magazine, May, 1991, courtesy of Michael Asher. Photograph by Tim Street-Porter.

Warhol and one of the first to buy a Roy Lichtenstein."[43] At that time she also bought her first cups by Ken Price, which inspired her to collect cups by other artists. During her lifetime her collection swelled to more than 500 examples and spilled over every surface in her house. Because of subsequent donations by the Betty M. Asher Estate, LACMA now owns more than 400, allowing for the serious study of this often whimsical form.

Asher's cups are primarily ceramic, although some are made of fur, birch bark, tar, crocheted wire, eggshells, straw, and laundry lint. Each cup liberally exploits the limitations of its vernacular and makes a unique comment on form, function, and context. Most were created by studio ceramists who veered away from the functional handled vessel and toward sculptural interpretation and wicked play. As Asher put it, "You wouldn't want to drink out of some of them, even if you could."[44] (The aesthetics of the contemporary teacup and its companion, the teapot, are discussed in the essay by Rebecca Niederlander herein, p. 195.)

By the mid-1980s, LACMA had acquired important core collections of vessels and cups and several significant large-scale ceramic sculptures. Like radiant navigational stars, these works guided the museum in its search to fill in the connections, to assemble a constellation of paradigmatic examples from major historical movements and acknowledged masters. The opportunity arose in 1987, when Howard and Gwen Laurie Smits offered LACMA their collection of contemporary ceramics. (For a profile of Gwen Laurie Smits, see p. 241.)

Private collections are structured along individual lines, accountable only to personal taste. Mrs. Smits described her own interests in an interview in 1984: "Through my lifetime it has been the vessel I have enjoyed.... I think I want things that I can handle.... I want to touch them and move them, enjoy them and share my interest with friends.... I limit myself to the contemporary, that is, by people who are still alive."[45] Mrs. Smits, who said in the same interview that she would find it "hard to stop" collecting, fits the description of the "true collector" described by Walter Benjamin: "The most profound enchantment for the collector is the thrill of acquisition.... The period, the region, the craftsmanship, the former ownership for a true collector, the whole background of an item adds up to a magic encyclopedia whose quintessence is the fate of his object."[46]

Magdalene Odundo, Kenya, active England, b. 1950.

Opposite, left:
Vessel #11, 1995. Red earthenware, hand built, burnished, and reduction fired. H.: 22 in. Smits Ceramics Purchase Fund. AC1995.90.1.

Opposite, right:
Charcoal-Burnished Pot, 1983. Terra-cotta, burnished and reduction fired. H.: 13 in. Gift of Howard and Gwen Laurie Smits. M.87.1.119.

Roseline Delisle, Canada, active
United States, b. 1952.

Top:
Triptyque 4A, 1986. Porcelain. H.: 12 in.
Gift of Howard and Gwen Laurie
Smits. M.87.1.35a–b.

Left:
Quadruple 3, 1990. Porcelain. H.: 21 in.
Howard Kottler Testamentary Trust.
AC1996.43.1.1–.2.

Right:
Study by Roseline Delisle.

Roseline Delisle, Canada, active United States, b. 1952. *8=1* (two views), 1997. Earthenware. H.: 52¾ in. Purchased with funds provided by Friends of Clay and Decorative Arts Council. AC1998.91.1.1–.2.

Eventually, the Smitses decided to donate the collection to a public institution, where it could be seen by an ever-widening circle and used as a resource for the study of contemporary ceramics. Collectors are often on the front lines of acquiring important works of their time, as they are able to follow and quickly respond to the art market. As art historian Susan M. Pearce explains, private patronage is essential to the vitality of a museum: "Characteristically much of the material culture of the past comes in groups which have been gathered together by a single individual....The transfer from formally private to formally public...is an important aspect of collection making."[47]

A small exhibition, *Contemporary Ceramics from the Smits Collection,* was held on the occasion of the donation, and a catalogue of the collection was published in 1990. Author Martha Drexler Lynn, then assistant curator of decorative arts, described the goals that governed LACMA's selection of the 190 objects in the Smits gift: to represent both Southern Californian and European, particularly British, potters (Mrs. Smits had acquired a significant portion of her collection in England); to reflect the influence and traditions of generations and cultural movements on one another; to capture techniques or moments; and to include new artists.[48]

The primary strength of the Smits Collection lies in its historical pieces by the pioneers of the new idiom of expressive works in clay, including the California-based ceramists Laura Andreson (1902–1999), Vivika and Otto Heino (1910–1995 and b. 1915), Glen Lukens (1887–1967), Harrison McIntosh (b. 1914), Gertrud and Otto Natzler (1908–1971 and b. 1908), Peter Voulkos (b. 1924), and Beatrice Wood (1894–1998); the British studio potters Lucie Rie (1902–1995), Hans Coper (1920–1981), and Michael Cardew (1901–1983); and the Japanese potter Shōji Hamada (1894–1978). (The important contributions made by many of these pioneering ceramists are addressed in the essay by Susan Peterson herein, p. 87.)

View of the exhibition *Contemporary Ceramics from the Smits Collection,* held on the occasion of the Smitses' gift, LACMA, 1987.

Lidya Buzio, Uruguay, b. 1948. *Roofscape* (front [top] and back), 1983. Earthenware. H.: 15½ in. Gift of Howard and Gwen Laurie Smits. M.87.1.20.

Christopher Gustin, United States,
b. 1952. *Pink Vessel,* 1986. Stoneware.
H.: 20½ in. Gift of Howard and Gwen
Laurie Smits. M.87.1.53.

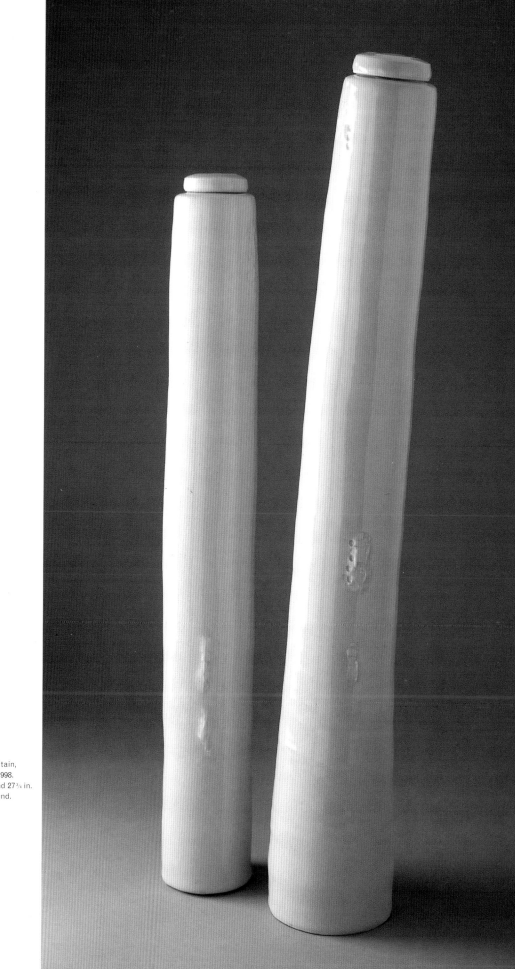

Edmund De Waal, Great Britain,
b. 1964. *Pair Tall Lidded Jars,* 1998.
Porcelain. H.: 23¾ in. (left) and 27¾ in.
Smits Ceramics Purchase Fund.
AC1999.67.1–.2.

Mineo Mizuno, Japan, active United States, b. 1944. *Two Orbs,* 1988. Whiteware. Black-and-white orb diam.: 24 in. Red orb diam.: 8 in. Promised gift of Lynn and Jerry Myers. TR.12732.15.1–.2.

Richard DeVore, United States, b. 1933.
Untitled #876, 1998. Earthenware. H.: 17 in.
Gift of Frank Lloyd Gallery, Santa Monica,
California, and Max Protetch, New York.
AC1999.39.1.

The Smits Collection's second great strength is its range of representative works by the leading second-generation artists, both U.S. and European, who in the 1980s used the vessel form as a point of departure. These artists, among them Alison Britton (b. 1948), Lidya Buzio (b. 1948), Roseline Delisle (b. 1952), Richard DeVore (b. 1933), Rick Dillingham (b. 1952), Wayne Higby (b. 1943), Magdalene Odundo (b. 1950), Martin Smith (b. 1950), and Betty Woodman (b. 1930), create pieces that retain an implied relationship to the container but jettison any notion of function in favor of other sculptural and structural considerations. The form of the vessel is essentially one of hollowness. As critic Jeff Perrone puts it, "a vessel...openly declares itself to be more void than form, a shell around nothing, a surround of emptiness."[49] Therefore, the vessel becomes a metaphor for the physicality of space, for the containment of context rather than content. Alison Britton's composed and constructed pots of angular volumes brushstroked with painterly splashes of glazes are studies in deconstruction; her geometric forms simultaneously engage spatiality and dematerialize it through the flatness of the surface decoration (p. 46). Wayne Higby's large landscape bowls speak of transmutations of space and time; the abstracted landscapes portrayed contiguously on interior and exterior are displaced and reconfigured according to shifting points of view (pp. 46 and 60). Magdalene Odundo's curvaceous and gestural vases are metaphors for the voluptuous female figure, refined and adorned (p. 33). Betty Woodman's nonfunctional containers of boldly exaggerated forms, surfaced with luscious, flowing glazes, are meditations on use as defined by presentation and aesthetic appeal (right and p. 47). These and other artists moved the vessel to new levels of meaning and transcendence through extensive manipulation of materials and the intellectualization of form.

Betty Woodman, United States, b. 1930. *Wall Piece,* 1982. Whiteware. H.: 17 ½ in. Gift of Gay B. Odmark. AC1992.296.1.1–.2.

Critic Mac McCloud (also known as the ceramic artist Mac McClain) reviewed the Smits collection glowingly: "A hierarchy of profoundly traditional values, refinement, expert studio research and authoritative craft is convincingly illuminated here." He concluded with an appeal: "I hope that future acquisitions by the Los Angeles County Museum of Art will augment this collection and clarify the vital evolution of clay during this recent and intense period of history."[50] He thus predicted LACMA's plan for the remaining decade of the millennium, a plan facilitated by the Smits Ceramics Purchase Fund, which Howard and Gwen Laurie Smits established to ensure the continued viability and growth of the collection.

Below, left:
Henry Pim, Great Britain, b. 1947. *Vessel,* 1987. Stoneware. H.: 21 in. Promised gift of Lynn and Jerry Myers. TR.12732.16.

Below, right:
Philip Maberry, United States, b. 1951. *Sister Dimension,* 1992. Earthenware. H.: 24 in. Promised gift of Lynn and Jerry Myers. TR.12732.12.1.–4.

William Daley, United States, b. 1925.
Bowman's Rest (two views), 1989.
Stoneware, unglazed. W.: 26½ in. Gift of
Howard and Gwen Laurie Smits in honor
of LACMA's twenty-fifth anniversary.
M.90.82.10.

Background:
Study for *Bowman's Rest* by William Daley.

Left:
Ewen Henderson, Great Britain, b. 1934.
Torso Form, 1988. Stoneware laminated
with porcelain and bone china. H.: 22 in.
Promised gift of Lynn and Jerry Myers.
TR.12732.10.

Below:
Sara Radstone, Great Britain, b. 1955.
Untitled, 1987. Stoneware. H.: 12 in.
Gift of Howard and Gwen Laurie Smits
in honor of LACMA's twenty-fifth
anniversary. M.90.82.41.

Above, left:
Alison Britton, Great Britain, b. 1948.
Two-Part Vessel, 1987. Earthenware.
H.: 11¾ in. (left side) and 13 in. Gift of
Howard and Gwen Laurie Smits in honor
of LACMA's twenty-fifth anniversary.
M.90.82.3 a, b.

Above, right:
Rick Dillingham, United States, b. 1952.
Black-and-White Sphere Vase, 1980.
Whiteware and silver leaf, hand gilt and
fired. Diam.: 10 in. Gift of Howard and
Gwen Laurie Smits. M.87.1.40.

Wayne Higby, United States, b. 1943.
Flat Rock Falls, 1979. Red earthenware,
raku fired. W.: 19 in. Purchased with
funds provided by Howard and Gwen
Laurie Smits. M.90.4.

Betty Woodman, United
States, b. 1930. *Pillow Pitcher,*
1983. Earthenware. H.: 20 in. Gift
of Howard and Gwen Laurie
Smits. M.87.1.184.

Karen Koblitz, United States, b. 1951.
Still-Life with Pitcher and Hedge Apple, 1985.
Low-fire ceramics with underglaze and clear
glaze. W.: 13½ in. Gift of Howard and Gwen
Laurie Smits. M.87.1.71a–b.

Background:
Study for a still life by Karen Koblitz.

Walter Keeler, Great Britain, b. 1942. *Tall Grey Pitcher,* c. 1983. Stoneware, wheel thrown, assembled, salt glazed, and reduction fired. H.: 13¾ in. Gift of Howard and Gwen Laurie Smits. M.87.1.68.

Jennifer Lee, Great Britain, b. 1956. *Pair of Asymmetric Dark Pots, Haloed Bands, Tilted Rim,* 1984. Colored stoneware, hand built. H.: 13¾ in. (left) and 9¾ in. Gift of Howard and Gwen Laurie Smits. M.87.1.75 and M.87.1.76.

Opposite:
Elsa Rady, United States, b. 1943. *Lily Still Life II,* 1989. Porcelain and sandblasted aluminum shelf. H.: 19 in. Smits Ceramics Purchase Fund, and donated in memory of Marvin R. Cole, courtesy of Holly Solomon Gallery, New York. M.91.168a–d.

Claudi Casanovas, Spain, b. 1956.
Circular Plate, 1994. Stoneware and
mixed media. Diam.: 24 in. Smits
Ceramics Purchase Fund. AC1999.66.1.

A Glimpse of the Coming Century

The dictum of the 1990s for the contemporary ceramics collection has been internationalism
and pluralism. As the world becomes a global village, centers of art activity become moving
targets rather than fixed locales, creating a fluid network of talented ceramists carrying on
a dialogue that can be transmitted almost instantaneously. LACMA recently enriched its
holdings with many outstanding examples of work created by ceramists around the world,
notably the super-refined wood-fired porcelain arrangement *Still Life with Two Teapots,* 1997
(opposite), by Australian artist Gwyn Hanssen Pigott (b. 1935); the large, sharply pierced and
scarred porcelain bowl *Manifestation of Dance,* 1990–1996 (p. 55), by the British-born Nigerian
artist Lawson Oyekan (b. 1961), an aesthetic expression of the scarification rituals of Oyekan's
Yoruban culture; and the raw and forceful *Circular Plate,* 1994 (above) by Catalonian ceramist
Claudi Casanovas (b. 1956), its rough surface reminiscent of Catalan hillsides. A continuing
goal of the collection is to acquire prominent work from all continents to enable the study
of the intellectual and creative connections across the world of ceramics.

Opposite:
Gwyn Hanssen Pigott, Australia, b. 1935.
Still Life with Two Teapots, 1997. Porcelain,
wood fired. H: from 2⅛ in. to 9¾ in. Smits
Ceramics Purchase Fund. AC1998.92.1.1–.14.

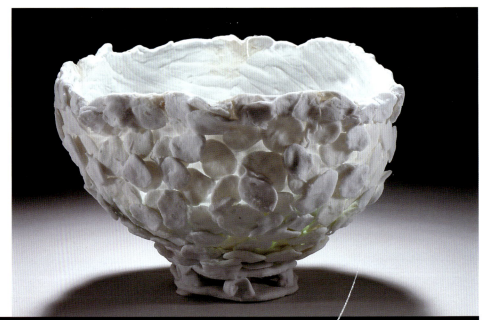

Mary Rogers, Great Britain, b. 1929. *Kiwi Bowl*, 1980s. Porcelain. H.: 5 in. Gift of Howard and Gwen Laurie Smits. M.87.1.141.

Top:
Rudolf Staffel, United States, b. 1911. *Light-Gatherer*, 1989. Porcelain with copper-oxide wash. W.: 9 in. Smits Ceramics Purchase Fund. AC1997.91.1–.2.

Right:
John Ward, Great Britain, b. 1938. *Striped Bowl*, c. 1983. Stoneware, hand built. W.: 9½ in. Gift of Howard and Gwen Laurie Smits. M.87.1.177.

Lawson Oyekan, Great Britain, b. 1961. *Manifestation of Dance,* 1990–96. Porcelain. Diam.: 21 in. Smits Ceramics Purchase Fund. AC1997.98.1.

Tony Marsh, United States, b. 1954. *Perforated Vessel,* 1996. Ceramic. W.: 22 in. Howard Kottler Testamentary Trust. AC1996.43.4.1–.14.

Geert Lap, Holland, b. 1951.

Untitled (Vessel), 1989. Stoneware, terra
sigillata. H.: 11 ½ in. Gift of Howard and
Gwen Laurie Smits. TR.12724.

Opposite:
Magenta Diptych, 1986. Stoneware, glazed.
H.: 5½ in. (left) and 18¼ in. Gift of Garth
Clark and Mark del Vecchio. M.91.129a–b.

Clockwise from above:
Brother Thomas Bezanson,
Canada, b. 1929. *Vase, Flask Form:
Hunan Tenmoku,* 1988. Porcelain with
oil-spot glaze. H.: 16½ in. Gift in honor
of Sadye Pucker by Sue and Bernie
Pucker. AC1996.74.1.1–.2.

Albert Green, United States,
1915–1994. *Bottlevase,* 1980.
Stoneware. H.: 12 in. Gift of Richard
and Margaret Kavesh. M.91.280.

Christine Jones, Great Britain,
b. 1955. *Vessel,* 1996. Earthenware.
H.: 10½ in. Gift of Marc and Diane
Grainer. AC1999.107.1.

Top, left:
Bodil Manz, Denmark, b. 1943. *Cylinder with Blue Lines,* 1996. Porcelain, cast, with high-fire transfers. Diam.: 9 in. Smits Ceramics Purchase Fund. AC1997.39.2.

Gordon Baldwin, OBE, Great Britain, b. 1932. *Egg on Base,* c. 1984. Earthenware. H.: 15 in. Gift of Howard and Gwen Laurie Smits. M.87.1.14.

Left:
Gustavo Perez, Mexico, b. 1950. *Untitled (Vaso Ovalado),* 1999. Stoneware. H.: 11½ in. Gift of Frank Lloyd Gallery, Santa Monica, California. TR.12815.

Jean-François Fouilhoux, France, b. 1947.
Sève, 1999. Stoneware with celadon glaze.
W.: 19 in. Gift of Galerie b15, Munich. TR.12855.
Photograph by Jean-Jacques Morer, courtesy
of Galerie b15.

Opposite:
Wayne Higby, United States,
b. 1943. *Lake Powell Memory—
Seven Mile Canyon,* 1996.
Porcelain, reduction fired, with
celadon glaze. W.: 22 in. Smits
Ceramics Purchase Fund.
AC1997.91.1.1–.4.

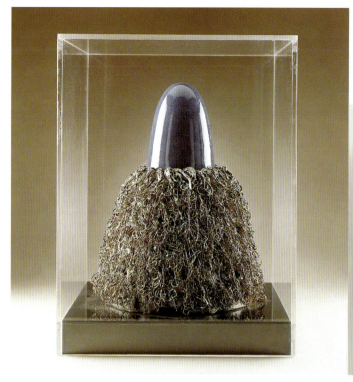

In 1994 LACMA celebrated Adrian Saxe, its own "global potter" (an appellation given by critic Christopher Knight),[51] in a midcareer retrospective (*The Clay Art of Adrian Saxe,* November 11, 1993, to January 30, 1994). This exhibition, curated by Martha Drexler Lynn, surveyed nearly one hundred works from 1967 to 1992. Knight had already claimed Saxe as L.A.'s very own "village potter" in his interview with the artist in 1991: "Every village has to have at least one, and Saxe is ours." Knight went on to explain his concept of the global village and pottery's position in this changed cultural environment: "No longer rural and organized around farming, the village today is urban and suburban in bearing, industrial and postindustrial in composition, unbound in its interconnections. Consequently, the idea of the clay pot, as a handmade, utilitarian necessity, no longer holds."[52] Saxe agreed and described the artist's role in this newly defined context: "I'm in a global village, so we have to have new kinds of potters. This is not tribal village art." Saxe has continually addressed the issue of utility in his work, producing highly decorative vessels that can function on many different levels. "There are all kinds of traditions of use," he has explained. "The function of objects doesn't have to be utilitarian. They are decorative objects. They increase the information present in the room, and they're visually integrated with the rooms they exist in. Their function—what they hold—is information."[53]

Saxe has deep roots in his village. He grew up in Los Angeles County (Glendale) and attended the Chouinard Art Institute in downtown Los Angeles from 1965 to 1969, ultimately receiving his BFA in 1974 from Chouinard's later incarnation, California Institute of the Arts, in Valencia. He has chaired the Ceramics Department at the University of California, Los Angeles, since 1973.

Geography is one of the subjects Saxe uses to engage the viewer, and his objects abound in visual pluralism. The vessels in his retrospective combined decorative embellishments mined from diverse cultures and episodes of ceramic history, reflecting, as Jim Collins puts it, "any number of national styles and symbolic forms, from ancient Chinese to neoclassical French to contemporary flea market."[54]

Consider *Cacaesthesia,* 1992 (opposite), a work in the retrospective that LACMA later acquired through the Smits Ceramics Purchase Fund. The stepped, footed base covered in ceramic gold luster imitates the ormolu (gilt bronze) mounts applied to traditional Chinese vases by Parisian designers in the eighteenth century to suit the tastes of the elite. The rich golden glaze refers to court porcelain presentation pieces typical of the Neoclassical production of the French Sèvres Manufactory. The antique tassel recalls the bygone era of Victorian niceties. The desiccated lemon, the flaccid form of the limp gourd folded over onto itself, and indeed the title (derived from *cacaoesthesia,* meaning morbidity) suggest anxieties about sexual dysfunction, decay, and death.

Saxe's fluid mingling of signs, symbols, and data from sources as divergent as *historica esoterica* and hip-hop pop culture represents a strategy he plans to continue: "I want to work to get richer, snottier, drawing from more obscure and esoteric sources, while discovering the structures to make them easily accessible. I want to push my intellectual understanding of art as far as possible without becoming academic. I want to push the process as far as possible without becoming pedantic. I want to retain the traditional format I use and yet find an avant-garde edge for it. I want to live in two contrasting worlds. It's a bit like driving with one foot on the brake, the other on the accelerator. It's a tough, urgent way to drive, but if you can afford the rubber, it's one hell of a way to move down the road."[55]

Opposite:
Adrian Saxe, United States, b. 1943. *Cacaesthesia,* 1992. Porcelain, stoneware, copper luster, dessicated lemon, and antique tassel. H.: 12¾ in. Smits Ceramics Purchase Fund. AC1993.35.1.1–.2.

Above, left:
Anne Hirondelle, United States, b. 1944. *Mime Diptych,* 1990. Stoneware. H.: 16 in. Purchased with funds provided by Sonny and Gloria Kamm. AC1998.57.1.1–.3.

Above, right:
Study by Anne Hirondelle.

Left:
Bennett Bean, United States, b. 1941. *Untitled (Double Series),* 1998. White earthenware and black slip, pit-fired, with acrylic and silver leaf. W.: 25 in. Gift of Katherine Bao Bean. AC1999.76.1.1–.3.

Gordon Baldwin, OBE, Great Britain, b. 1932. *Perched Vessel,* 1985. Earthenware. Height: 43 13/16 in. Promised gift of Linda Leonard Schlenger. TR.12720.1.1–.2.

Saxe's retrospective, moored to cross-cultural vocabularies, tinkering with conventions of use, commented on complex social issues related to the value, status, and display of decorative arts objects. The work questioned the traditional view that a well-crafted clay pot should be judged against the exacting standards of William Morris, the nineteenth-century Arts and Crafts theoretician and practitioner who advocated "honesty to materials," and Bernard Leach, the early twentieth-century potter and philosopher whose motto was "beauty in utility."[56] It asked the viewer to evaluate again the abiding prejudice against the material itself. Could an object made of inexpensive, common clay be considered art? Does that object become more valuable if lavishly gilded and encrusted with semiprecious stones? Knight eloquently summarized the pleasures and challenges of Saxe's work: "With outrageous humor and unspeakable beauty, he makes intensely seductive objects that exploit traditional anthropomorphic qualities associated with ceramics. Having pressed the question of the utility of his own art in a post-industrial world, his work engages us in a dialogue about our own place in a radically shifting cultural universe."[57]

In addition to geographical pluralism, LACMA's ceramics collection in the 1990s has been governed by pluralism of form, based on the recognition that collections of contemporary ceramics should include sculptures as well as vessels. The production of both vessel and sculptural work in clay has been going on for millennia, as demonstrated by artifacts from around the world. It seems arbitrary to separate the traditions in the twentieth century based on prejudicial considerations of scale or intent. Parity in numbers is not the goal; the collection can retain its focus on vessels while broadening its scope to encompass representative sculptures by key artists.

The earliest sculptural acquisitions, the expressionistic works by Voulkos and the installation sculptures by Mason and Price, were complemented later by a superb iconic-sardonic portrait bust, *Way West of Athens,* 1983 (p. 167), by Robert Arneson (1930–1992), the father of Funk, and a fantastical figurative work by Elaine Carhartt (b. 1951), *Queen,* 1980 (p. 171). This grouping has been further enhanced with signature sculptures by many of the acclaimed masters, including Robert Brady (b. 1946), Stephen De Staebler (b. 1933), Viola Frey (b. 1933), Jun Kaneko (b. 1942), Michael Lucero (b. 1953), Richard Shaw (b. 1941), and Toshiko Takaezu (b. 1922). The contemporary figurative tradition is discussed at length in the essay by Peter Selz herein, p. 159.

Opposite:
Kurt Weiser, United States, b. 1950. *Bird Call,* 1998. Porcelain. H.: 18½ in. Purchased with funds provided by Friends of Clay and Decorative Arts Council. AC1998.91.2.1–.2.

Background:
Study by Kurt Weiser.

Kate Malone, Great Britain, b. 1959.
Triple Heart Pod: Love Grows, 1998.
Stoneware, coiled, hand built, and
crystalline glazed. W.: 22¾ in.
Purchased with funds provided by the
Decorative Arts Council. TR.12832.

Opposite:
Michael Sherrill, United
States, b. 1954. *Turning Leaves
(Set of Nine Bottles),* 1998.
Stoneware with alkaline glaze.
H.: from 9½ in. to 31½ in. Gift
of Gump's San Francisco.
AC1999.78.1.1–.9.

David Regan, United States, b. 1964.
Deer Tureen, 1996. Porcelain. W.: 27 in.
Promised gift of Anne B. and Marvin H.
Cohen. Photograph © Anthony Cuñha.

Mara Superior, United States, b. 1951.
Abundance (Tureen), 1996. Porcelain.
H.: 17 ½ in. Gift of Melinda M. Sullivan and
Paul R. C. Sullivan. AC1999.77.1.1–.3.

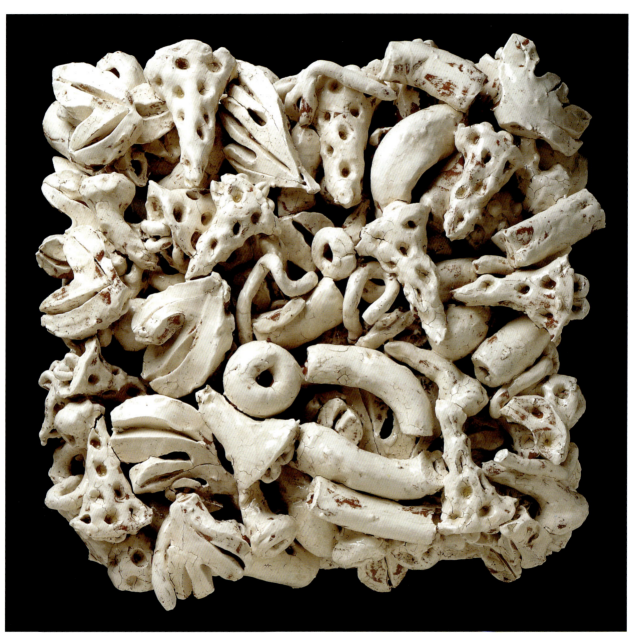

Annabeth Rosen, United States, b. 1957.
Packed Tile, White, 1998. Red clay with
white slip under lead glaze. W.: 23½ in. Gift
of Dorothy Weiss Gallery. TR.12752.2.

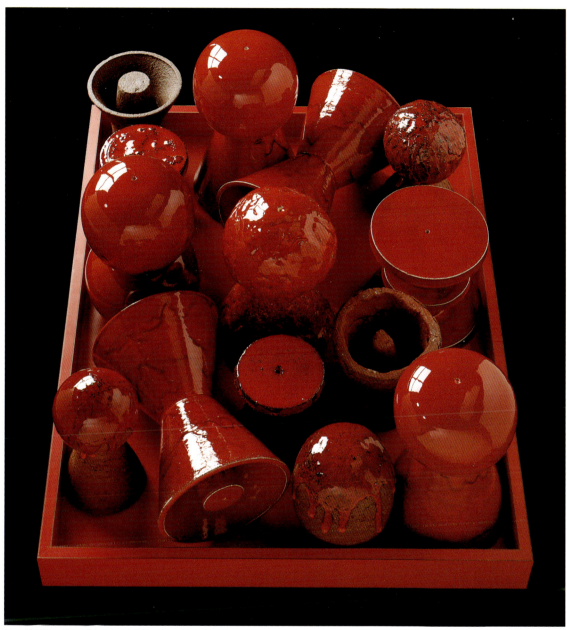

Tony Hepburn, Great Britain, active United
States, b. 1942. *Red Tray,* 1998. Ceramic and
Formica. W.: 23¼ in. Purchased with funds
provided by Lois and Bob Boardman.
AC1999.29.1–.15.

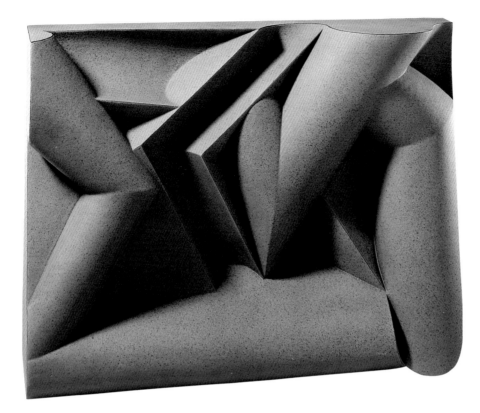

"What You See Is What You See": A Defining Moment for the Twenty-First Century

According to the contemporary painter Frank Stella, when you stand
before a work of art, "What you see is what you see."[58] In other words, the
object itself must communicate, directly and completely, the artist's intention and vision. The experience is most rewarding when works of art are
formally challenging and visually entrancing.

The more than two hundred and seventy-five ceramic objects that
have been assembled and selected for the exhibition *Color and Fire:
Defining Moments in Studio Ceramics, 1950–2000,* present the viewer with
the opportunity to establish this direct dialogue and to participate in
the enriched sensory experience of viewing ceramics in the context of a
museum environment. The spectrum of artistic expression ranges from the
classical to the cutting edge, embodied in intimately scaled, beautifully
profiled pots (pretty, humble, elegant), weighty sculptural pots (organic,
volumetric, gestural, architectonic), and monumental freestanding sculptures (figurative, abstract, nonobjective). This broad sampling demonstrates

the diversity, energy, and inventiveness of the expanded field of ceramics as a contemporary art form. This embrace of both traditional and vanguard work presents a balanced and comprehensive view, illustrating the breadth of contemporary responses to the challenge of making ceramics in the late twentieth century. Our hope is that the exhibition and catalogue of *Color and Fire* will mark the first defining moment of the new millennium.

Robert Winokur, United States, b. 1933. *Italian Hill Town,* n.d. Pennsylvania brick clay, salt glazed, with slips and engobes. W.: 24½ in. Gift of Helen Drutt, Philadelphia, and the artist. TR.12834.2.1–.2.

Jo Lauria, assistant curator of decorative arts at LACMA, organized the exhibition *Color and Fire: Defining Moments in Studio Ceramics, 1950–2000.* She holds an MFA from Otis College of Art and Design, an MA from Loyola Marymount University, Los Angeles, and a BA in art history from Yale University. Specializing in modern and contemporary decorative arts, she oversees the museum's collection of furniture, ceramics, glass, wood, and metal and has published and lectured extensively in the field of decorative arts. Previous shows she has helped organize at LACMA include *Common Forms, High Art: Three Centuries of American Furniture; Designing Modernity: The Arts of Reform and Persuasion, 1885–1945;* and *L.A. Modern and Beyond: Modernist and Postmodernist Furniture and Decorative Art.*

Paula Winokur, United States, b. 1935. *Excavation:
Site 1,* 1990. Porcelain, slab constructed, cast vessel,
metallic sulfates. W.: 32 in. Gift of Helen Drutt,
Philadelphia, and the artist, in honor of Lois and
Robert Boardman. TR.12534.1.1.

Nancy Selvin, United States, b. 1943. *Still-Life Bottle Collection #4,* 1998. Ceramic on wood shelf. Shelf w.: 46½ in. Gift of Nancy Selvin and courtesy of Sybaris Gallery, Royal Oak, Michigan. TR.12689.

Left:
Ralph Bacerra, United States, b. 1938. *Untitled Cloud Vessel,* 1997. Porcelain. H.: 19½ in. Purchased with funds provided by Friends of Clay and Decorative Arts Council Fund. AC1998.91.3.1–.3.

Opposite, left:
Anna Silver, United States, b. 1932. *Untitled Vessel,* 1997. Earthenware with glazes. H.: 26 in. Gift of Frank Lloyd Gallery, Santa Monica, California. AC1999.103.1.

Opposite, right:
Andrea Gill, United States, b. 1948. *Spiral Jar,* 1982. Earthenware. H.: 24 in. Gift of Howard and Gwen Laurie Smits in honor of LACMA's twenty-fifth anniversary. M.90.82.16.

Patti Warashina, United States, b. 1940. *Yellow Ford from the East*, 1988. Low-fire whiteware with underglaze, wood cord, in glass vitrine. Vitrine w.: 39½ in. Sculpture w.: 32 in. Purchased with funds provided by Lois and Bob Boardman, and gift of Decorative Arts Council in Memory of Maggie Omerberg. TR.12721.1

Notes

1   See *Artists of Los Angeles and Vicinity,* exh. cat. (Los Angeles: Los Angeles County Museum of Art, 1957).

2   "Voulkos Exhibits New Stoneware," *Craft Horizons* 16, no. 3 (May/June 1956): 47.

3   See *Artists of Los Angeles and Vicinity 1958 Annual Exhibition,* exh. cat. (Los Angeles: Los Angeles County Museum of Art, 1958), and *Artists of Los Angeles and Vicinity 1959 Annual Exhibition,* exh. cat. (Los Angeles: Los Angeles County Museum of Art, 1959).

4   Rose Slivka, an authority on Voulkos's work, discusses this series of sixteen large-scale sculptures he created in 1958 and 1959, after mastering the technique of creating monumentality in clay. See *The Art of Peter Voulkos: Retrospective,* exh. cat. (Tokyo: Sezon Museum of Art, 1995), 32.

5   Thomas W. Leavitt, *Peter Voulkos: Sculpture/Painting/Ceramics,* exh. cat. (Los Angeles: Felix Landau Gallery, 1959), unpag.

6   See Rose Slivka and Karen Tsujimoto, *The Art of Peter Voulkos* (New York: Kodansha International in collaboration with Oakland Museum, 1995), 42.

7   Many writers and critics have devoted considerable research to chronicling this "revolution" in ceramics. For a general discussion see Garth Clark, *American Ceramics: 1876 to the Present* (New York: Abbeville, 1987), chaps. 8 and 9; and Elaine Levin, "Abstract Expressionism: Its Effects and Ramifications, 1955–1965," part 5 of *The History of American Ceramics: 1607 to the Present* (New York: Harry N. Abrams, 1988). For a more current discussion see Mary Davis MacNaughton, "Innovation in Clay: The Otis Era, 1954–1960," in *Revolution in Clay: The Marer Collection of Contemporary Ceramics* (Claremont, Calif.: Ruth Chandler Williamson Gallery, Scripps College; Seattle and London: University of Washington Press, 1994).

8   Rose Slivka, "The New Ceramic Presence," *Craft Horizons* 21, no. 4 (July/August 1961): 35.

9   Ibid.

10 Harold Rosenberg, "The American Action Painters," *Art News* 51, no. 8 (December 1952): 22–23, 48–50.

11 Nancy Marmer, "Los Angeles," *Artforum* 3, no. 10 (June 1965): 9–11.

12 John Coplans, "The Sculpture of John Mason," in *John Mason: Sculpture,* exh. cat ([Los Angeles: Los Angeles County Museum of Art, 1966]), unpag.

13 For a perspective on the importance of Coplans's contribution see Garth Clark and Margie Hughto, "1960," in *A Century of Ceramics in the United States, 1878–1978* (New York: E. P. Dutton in association with Everson Museum of Art, 1979), 157–81.

14 John Coplans, *Abstract Expressionist Ceramics,* exh. cat. (Irvine, Calif.: Art Gallery, University of California, Irvine, 1966), 7.

15 Ibid., 13.

16 See, e.g., Helen Giambruni, "Exhibitions: John Mason," *Craft Horizons* 27, no. 1 (January/February 1967): 38–40; Judith Wechsler, "Los Angeles: John Mason," *Artforum* 5, no. 6 (February 1967): 65, ill. p. 64; Jules Langsner, "Los Angeles," *Art News* 65, no. 9 (January 1967): 26; and William Wilson, "In the Galleries: Great Talent in Huge Sculptures," *Los Angeles Times,* 28 November 1966, part 4, p. 7.

17 Helen Giambruni makes this statement in her review for *Craft Horizons,* p. 39, and John Mason has confirmed it, interview with the author, 22 June 1999.

18 Giambruni, ibid.

19 Unpublished transcript from "Revolution of the Wheel," prod. Kathleen Garfield, 4 February 1994.

20 For a detailed history of the Natzlers' career see "Chronology," comp. Ursula Ilse-Neuman, in *Gertrud and Otto Natzler: Collaboration/Solitude,* exh. cat. (New York: American Craft Museum, 1993), 65–83.

21 See Gregor Norman-Wilcox, introduction to *The Ceramic Work of Gertrud and Otto Natzler: A Retrospective Exhibition,* exh. cat. (Los Angeles: Los Angeles County Museum of Art, 1966), unpag.

22 Otto Natzler, preface to *The Ceramic Work of Gertrud and Otto Natzler,* unpag.

23 Rose Henderson, "Natzler Ceramics," *The Studio* 153, no. 766 (January 1957): 18–21.

24 Rose A. Sperry, preface to *Gertrud and Otto Natzler Ceramics: Catalogue of the Collection of Mrs. Leonard M. Sperry, and a Monograph by Otto Natzler* (Los Angeles: Los Angeles County Museum of Art, 1968), unpag.

25 Ken Price quoted in Susan Wechsler, *Low-Fire Ceramics: A New Direction in American Clay* (New York: Watson-Guptill, 1981), 115.

26 The Ferus Gallery, the joint venture of assemblage artist Edward Keinholz and celebrated curator Walter Hopps, opened to the public on 15 March 1957. The objective of the newly aligned art dealers was to bring together "the best younger artists in the Southern California region as a group... [this] vital group of artists of the highest ambition who lived and worked in California" (James Monte, foreword to *Late Fifties at the Ferus,* exh. cat. [Los Angeles: Los Angeles County Museum of Art, 1968]). Kienholz and Hopps left the gallery in the fall of 1958, and Irving Blum and Sadye Moss took over until it closed its doors in 1966. Robert Irwin had one-person exhibitions at Ferus in 1959, 1960, 1962, and 1964. Two other ceramic artists, Jerry Rothman and Paul Soldner, who were students of Voulkos at Otis Art Institute, also exhibited their work at Ferus.

27 Ken Price quoted in Wechsler, 114.

28 Joan Simon, "An Interview with Ken Price," *Art in America* 68, no. 1 (January 1980): 98.

29 John Coplans, "Circle of Styles on the West Coast," *Art in America* 52, no. 3 (June 1964): 40.

30 Ibid, 40–41.

31 Kurt Von Meier, "Los Angeles Letter," *Art International* 10, no. 8 (20 October 1966): 45.

32 Walter Benjamin discusses this concept in "The Work of Art in the Age of Mechanical Reproduction," in *Illuminations,* ed. Hannah Arendt, trans. Harry Zohn (New York: Schocken Books, 1968).

33 Robert Williams, "Rubberneck Manifesto," in *Kustom Kulture: Von Dutch, Ed "Big Daddy" Roth, Robert Williams and Others,* exh. cat. (Laguna Beach, Calif.: Laguna Art Museum in association with Last Gasp of San Francisco, 1993), 71.

34 Lucy R. Lippard, "Ken Price," in *Robert Irwin/Kenneth Price,* exh. cat. (Los Angeles: Los Angeles County Museum of Art, 1966), unpag.

35 Ken Price quoted in Wechsler, 116.

36 Maurice Tuchman, introduction to *Ken Price: Happy's Curios,* exh. cat. (Los Angeles: Los Angeles County Museum of Art, 1978), 7.

37 Ibid, 8.

38 Ken Price, interview by Joan Simon, *Art in America* 68, no. 1 (January 1980): 98–104.

39 See Garth Clark, *American Potters: The Work of Twenty Modern Masters* (New York: Watson-Guptill, 1981): 46.

40 Peter Schjeldahl, *Artforum* 17, no. 3 (November 1978): 78–79.

41 Rose Slivka, "West Coast Ceramics," in *West Coast Ceramics,* exh. cat. (Amsterdam: Stedelijk Museum, 1979), 36.

42 Adrian Saxe quoted in Garth Clark, "Betty Asher 1914–1994," *American Craft* 54, no. 5 (October/ November 1994): 23.

43 Ibid.

44 Betty Asher quoted in Lisbet Nilson, "Queen of Cups—Betty Asher's Collection Fills Her Home to the Brim," *Angeles,* May 1991, 87.

45 Gwen Laurie Smits, interview by Jay Belloli, in *Contemporary Ceramic Vessels, Two Los Angeles Collections: The Betty Asher Collection, The Howard and Gwen Laurie Smits Collection,* exh. cat. (Pasadena, Calif.: Baxter Art Gallery, California Institute of Technology, 1984), 11–14.

46 Walter Benjamin, "Unpacking My Library," in *Illuminations,* 60.

47 Susan M. Pearce, *Museums, Objects and Collections: A Cultural Study* ([London]: Leicester University Press, 1992), 36.

48 Martha Drexler Lynn, "From Vessel to Vehicle: An Introduction," in *Clay Today: Contemporary Ceramists and Their Work; A Catalogue of the Howard and Gwen Laurie Smits Collection at the Los Angeles County Museum of Art* (Los Angeles: Los Angeles County Museum of Art; San Francisco: Chronicle Books, 1990), 10.

49 Jeff Perrone, "Exquisite/Coarse," in *Adrian Saxe,* exh. cat. (Kansas City, Mo.: Art Galleries, 1987), 7.

50 Mac McCloud, "A History of Clay," *Artweek,* 11 July 1987, 4.

51 Christopher Knight, "The Global Potter," *Los Angeles Times,* 24 November 1991, "Calendar" section, 92, 98.

52 Ibid., 92.

53 Adrian Saxe, interview by David Hoffman, *Kansas City Star,* 5 April 1987, 6D.

54 Jim Collins, "Adrian Saxe and the Postmodern Vessel," in Martha Drexler Lynn, *The Clay Art of Adrian Saxe* (Los Angeles: Los Angeles County Museum of Art; New York: Thames and Hudson, 1993), 123.

55 Adrian Saxe, interview by Garth Clark, *American Ceramics* 1, no. 4 (fall 1982): 28.

56 For a basic overview of Morris's philosophies, see *The Collected Letters of William Morris,* ed. Norman Kelvin (Princeton: Princeton University Press,1984); Eugene D. Lemire, *The Unpublished Lectures of William Morris* (Detroit: Wayne State University Press, 1969); and *Collected Works of William Morris* (London: Longmans Green, 1914). For more on Bernard Leach refer to his writings in *A Potter's Book* (London: Faber & Faber Ltd., 1940) and *Beyond East and West* (New York: Watson-Guptill, 1978); and for an overview of his philosophies see J. P. Hodin, *Bernard Leach: A Potter's Work* (London: Jupiter Books, 1977); and Bernard Leach, *The Potter's Challenge,* ed. David Outerbridge (New York: Dutton-Sunrise, 1975).

57 Christopher Knight, "The Human Value of California Clay: Adrian Saxe Uses and Undermines Tradition in LACMA Exhibition," *Los Angeles Times,* 13 November 1993, F1, F12.

58 William Rubin, *Frank Stella* (New York: Museum of Modern Art, 1970), 42.

Left:
Lizbeth Stewart, United States, b. 1948. *Cat and Snake,* 1990. Earthenware, hand built. H.: 37 in. Gift of Helen Drutt, Philadelphia, and the artist, in honor of Lois and Robert Boardman. TR.12834.3.1–.3

Opposite:
Toshiko Takaezu, United States (Hawaii), b. 1922. *Homage to Ko'olau Range* (detail), 1994–95. Stoneware, glazed. H.: 57 in. Gift of Karen Johnson Boyd. TR.12688. See p. 115 for full view.

Ceramics in the West

Shōji Hamada, Japan, 1894–1978. *Bottle,* 1955–60. Stoneware. H.: 9½ in. Smits Ceramics Purchase Fund. M.89.100.

Glen Lukens, United States, 1887–1957. *Plate,* 1940. Earthenware, glazed. Diam.: 15 in. Purchased with funds provided by Howard and Gwen Laurie Smits. M.89.74.

The Explosion of the 1950s

SUSAN PETERSON

Ceramics is so ancient an art that it is often difficult to find anything new, but the 1950s ceramics movement on the West Coast of the United States was definitely new. The stories of the original passion, uncommon determination and drive, and brilliance of the actors on the scene are alive in those of us who were there, and they have powerfully affected those who came after. The intense pace and vigor, the thrill of making astonishing discoveries, and the search for meaningful nonfunctional forms that characterized these vibrant times may never be repeated, although the search continues.

What we now call contemporary ceramics began in the 1950s in the studios of artists who, working in one-of-a-kind clay vessels and sculptures, set the stage for a major art form that eventually spread to the rest of the world. I was among this group, and although in retrospect it seems clear that we were part of a revolution, we weren't aware of it at the time. Instead, this new field was

Laura Andreson, United States, 1902–1999. *Brown Bowl with Projections,* 1983. Porcelain. Diam.: 9½ in. Gift of Howard and Gwen Laurie Smits. M.90.82.1.

Bernard Leach, China, active England; 1887–1979. *Bottle,* c. 1950. Stoneware. H.: 7½ in. Gift of Roy Rydell in memory of Bruce Anderson. AC1999.111.1.

Marguerite Wildenhain, France, 1896–1985. *Large Jar,* 1950s. Earthenware. H.: 9 in. Gift of Pauline Blank. AC1992.226.2.1–.2.

Bernard Leach in 1971. Photograph © Peter Kinnear, courtesy of Susan Peterson.

Bernard Leach, China, active England; 1887–1979. *Untitled (Vase),* 1946. Stoneware, glazed. Diam.: 8 in. Promised gift of Susan Peterson. TR.12889.

born of our trials and errors; our perseverance toward conceptual goals of form, color, and expression; spontaneity and fun; experimental wallowing in the clay; and the difficult technical tasks of building wheels and kilns capable of realizing our visions.

The groundwork for these innovations had been laid years earlier, in the first decades of the twentieth century, when a renewed interest in craft values helped to bring about the studio pottery movement in Europe and the United States. Potters began to work individually or in small workshops, making functional and decorative ware by hand, rather than in factories. Craftspeople moved away from Victorian opulence and toward a stricter sense of formal beauty, influenced by the William Morris movement in England, which first reinstated handcraft after the Industrial Revolution. Many potters also absorbed the impact on modern design of the Weimar Bauhaus School in Germany, which first gave us the ubiquitous slogan "form follows function." Independent from both these schools were Bernard Leach (1887–1979) and Shōji Hamada (1894–1978), two original thinkers who would become the most influential figures in the international studio pottery movement.

Shōji Hamada, Japan, 1894–1978. *Press-Moulded Reverse-Curve Bottle,* 1955–1960. Stoneware with cobalt and iron engobe and salt glaze. H.: 9¾ in. Gift of Laura Andreson. M.86.20.

Shōji Hamada, Japan, 1894–1978. *Press-Moulded Square Bottle,* 1955–60. Stoneware with khaiki over-glaze. H.: 9½ in. Gift of Laura Andreson. M.85.271.

Shōji Hamada at his compund in Mashiko, Japan, c. 1970. Photograph by Susan Peterson.

Jerome Ackerman, United States, b. 1920. *Uranus #1,* 1996. Stoneware, hand-thrown, reduction-fired, with carved decoration. Diam.: 10 in. Gift of Laura Ackerman in honor of her father, Jerome Ackerman. AC1996.208.1.

Hamada, a young Japanese who had studied ceramic art and was a graduate of a ceramic technical institute, and Leach, who had been raised in the Far East and was studying pottery in Japan, met in Tokyo in 1920 at an exhibition of Leach's pots. With the common goal of being artist potters, the two soon became friends. Hamada accompanied Leach to England, where they searched for clays and established a stoneware and porcelain pottery at St. Ives, Cornwall. While traveling the museums of the world, the two young men had also developed their own universal view of ceramics. With two Japanese compatriots, Sōetsu Yanagi and Kanjirō Kawai, they later coined the term *mingei,* roughly translated as folkcraft, to describe the work philosophy that they revered. Mingei honored the pottery and other arts of the anonymous or unknown artisans whose untutored lifelong efforts Leach and Hamada wanted to emulate. Paradoxically, by spreading an appreciation of unselfconscious folk art, they made the world gradually aware of the artists—including themselves—behind the pots.

Members of the American Ceramic Society, Southern California section, 1950s. Back row, from left: Peter Voulkos, Raul Coronel, Louisa and Albert King, Malcolm Leland, Jerome and Evelyn Ackerman, David Cressy. Middle row: Sue Shrode, Bernard Kester, Vivika Heino. Front row: John Harding, Otto Heino, John Mason, Susan Peterson. Copyright, 1950, *Los Angeles Times*. Reprinted by permission.

Before the 1950s, however, Leach and Hamada had more influence in Europe and Japan than in the United States, and few potters working in California knew their work or the philosophy that informed it. There was little communication among potters around the world in the first half of the century, and historically the western United States had few of the traditions of the East Coast. Since the arrival of the first European settlers in 1620, the East Coast had some traditions for low-fire earthenware and more for high-fire stoneware and porcelain (the three types of ceramic wares), as well as wheel-throwing and kiln facility. In contrast, the Mexican, Latin American, Native American, and Anglo culture of the West Coast had almost no high-fire pottery antecedents and very little knowledge of wheel throwing. In Southern California at midcentury, we fledgling artists cavalierly threw off these obstacles and struggled with new ideas that required innovative solutions to problems of fabrication and controlling huge firing chambers and temperature variables. This struggle was, in my view, a primary factor in the fifties ceramic explosion.

Southern California—with its sunshine, white-cloud and blue-sky brilliance, and pioneering urban development of the desert landscape—provided a fertile environment for the rebirth of clay. Buildings shaped to evoke their names (the hat of the Brown Derby, the orange of Orange Julius stands) vied with the architecture of Frank Lloyd Wright and the Greene brothers. By the 1950s about four hundred small potteries in Los Angeles were turning out pink flamingos, black panthers, surreys with fringes, and the like in figurines and dinnerware—a far cry from European crafts influenced by Bauhaus principles.

Laura Andreson, c. 1946, working in her studio at UCLA, above, and below right, c. 1975, in her house in Hollywood with a display of her pottery. Photographs by Imogen Cunningham, © 1978 The Imogen Cunningham Trust, all rights reserved, courtesy of Pauline Blank.

Above, right:
Laura Andreson, United States, 1902–1999. *Blue Bowl with Foot,* 1980. Porcelain, wheel thrown and glazed. Diam.: 10 in. Gift of Howard and Gwen Laurie Smits. M.87.1.8.

Below:
Studies by Laura Andreson, courtesy of Pauline Blank.

Glen Lukens at the University of Southern California, c. 1935. Photograph © Archives of American Art, Smithsonian Institution, Washington, D.C.

Below:
Glen Lukens, United States, 1887–1967. *Yellow Plate,* 1930. Earthenware. Diam.: 13 ½ in. Gift of Howard and Gwen Laurie Smits. M.87.1.85.

This playful, kitsch culture was what studio potters—many of them originally from Europe or other parts of the United States—found in California in the 1930s and 1940s. Laura Andreson, Glen Lukens, Carlton Ball, Marguerite Wildenhain, Gertrud and Otto Natzler, and Beatrice Wood, among others, explored techniques independently, exhibited their works, wrote books, and taught one another and their students what they'd discovered. Their techniques and methods would come to define the ceramics of this region before the 1950s.

Laura Andreson (1902–1999) began teaching ceramics at the University of California, Los Angeles, while still a student there in the thirties, finished a degree in art education at Columbia University in New York, and returned to complete a lifelong professional and artistic career in Southern California. At first she made low-fire earthenwares glazed in bright reds, yellows, and turquoise-greens, subdued by undercoats of dark iron oxide stains. She also created radiantly brilliant colors by modifying old Persian reduction-firing luster techniques. Years later she began making the porcelain, pastel, crystalline-surfaced bottles and bowls for which she became internationally known.

Andreson was a pioneer in unknown territory. With an insatiable zest for knowledge, she traveled the world to see museums and study the ceramic art of all time. She created works that were strong and beautiful and experimented with the entire clay vocabulary. She didn't know how to throw on the potter's wheel, so in 1947 she sent four graduate students to a Mills College summer session; after learning from Carlton Ball, they returned to teach her the skill. Andreson influenced a trail of followers through her work and her long career as a professor.

Glen Lukens (1887–1967), who founded the Ceramics Department at the University of Southern California in 1933, was a self-taught ceramist and innovative technologist who prospected his clay and glaze materials from the deserts of Palm Springs and Death Valley. Lukens pulverized agate, amethyst, turquoise, and other locally found stones, added glass powder, and produced decorative surfaces that became famous in the United States as "California colors."

Aesthetically ahead of his time with his simple, elegant forms, Lukens won first prize in the 1936 Ceramic National exhibition at the Everson Museum in Syracuse, New York, and was given the prestigious Binns Award for lifetime achievement from the National Ceramic Society in 1949. He taught many who became professional potters and teachers. Upon retiring from the University of Southern California, he worked in Haiti for several years, helping to replace gourds used to contain food with more sanitary clay vessels, which he taught his students there to hand-make and fire.

Carlton Ball, one of Lukens's students at USC, began teaching ceramics at Mills College in Oakland in 1939. At that time he was firing his clay work at earthenware temperatures but using a native clay from Northern California that required firing at 2200°F. to make it strong and dense. No artist working in California then understood ceramics technology enough to make proper use of the local clays. High-fire stoneware and porcelain would not be seen in the West for another ten years.

Ball was passionate about knowing more than he had been taught in college. He particularly wanted to throw on the potter's wheel, as he had seen it done in photographs. So he obtained a daily job demonstrating the skill he had not yet acquired, at the San Francisco World's Fair on Treasure Island in the summer of 1939. He built his own wooden kick wheel, patterned after German ones he had seen in pictures, and added a motor. He told me that he had the visitor's rope placed far away so that observers

could not see his mistakes, and that seated next to him coil-building pots every day was María Martínez, from San Ildefonso Pueblo in New Mexico, already the most famous Native American potter. After that summer Ball built more wheels, installed them at Mills College, and taught the first throwing classes in the West. His own skill became phenomenal. He threw extraordinarily large forms with classic profile lines, exhibited in the craft fairs, and wrote how-to articles for several decades in ceramics magazines.

In the early 1940s expatriate Marguerite Wildenhain (1896–1985) arrived from Vienna via Holland and the German Bauhaus School to live in Northern California. Wildenhain knew nothing of the materials or kilns in her new country. Carlton Ball helped her establish her studio at Pond Farm in Guerneville, California, on the picturesque Russian River, and gave her glaze batches to try, including one that she accidentally overfired, causing iron specks in the clay to bleed through. The look became a trademark from her first exhibition in 1946 at the prestigious Gumps Gallery in San Francisco.

Far left:
Marguerite Wildenhain at work in her studio at Pond Farm, Guerneville, California, c. 1940. Photograph © Otto Hagel Estate, courtesy of Archives of American Art, Smithsonian Institution, Washington, D.C.

Marguerite Wildenhain, France, 1896–1985. *Two-Handled Chalice,* c. 1940s. Earthenware. H.: 6 in. Gift of Roy Rydell in memory of Bruce Anderson. TR.12753.11.

Wildenhain came from a structured, European, apprentice-journeyman style of training, which she instituted in her summer workshops for students at Pond Farm. She was unimpressed with our offhand university and art-school teaching methods and denounced them vociferously at her first workshop, presented by Laura Andreson at the University of California, Los Angeles, in the early fifties. Wildenhain's first book, *Pottery: Form and Expression,* an impressive discussion of her philosophy of nature and of simple natural forms, made a distinct impact on many potters, especially those for whom throwing functional shapes on the wheel was as important as it was for her. At about the same time, Henry Varnum Poor, the well-known East Coast painter and potter, wrote the treatise *A Book of Pottery: From Mud to Immortality,* which both Wildenhain and Leach admired.

Wildenhain was an especially formidable mentor for ceramists such as Charles Counts, a native of Tennessee who teaches now in Africa; Hui Ka Kwong, who is best known for his brightly pigmented ceramic sculptures and for helping New York painter Roy Lichtenstein make the colored glazes for his dinnerware designs; and Harrison McIntosh (b. 1914), who at more than eighty years old still works in crisp simple forms with engobes and oxidation semimatte glazes and continues to design ceramics and glassware for manufacturers in Japan.

The Natzlers, Gertrud (1908–1971) and Otto (b. 1908), immigrated to California in 1938 from Austria and created a stir when they exhibited their distinctive cadmium-oxide, red and yellow glazes on delicately shaped pots at the Dalzell Hatfield Galleries in Los Angeles. Gertrud threw paper-thin bottles and bowls; in addition to creating brilliant colors, Otto concocted low-fire crystalline and lava-bursting textured glazes. They numbered as well as signed all of their one-of-a-kind works, conferring on each a unique importance.

Otto's experiments with aventurine gold-flecked glazes, as well as rock-surfaced harsh mattes and silicon-carbide-blistered coatings, necessitated firing experiments, too. He was one of the first potters to investigate low-temperature reduced-oxygen firing by inserting chunks of wood and mothballs into the electric kiln during the cooling cycle. Although Otto kept his methods secret, and few people had the opportunity to watch Gertrud's masterful throwing techniques, the couple's work influenced many artists, including Beatrice Wood.

Wood, who died in 1998 at age 105, was a legend in her own time. Born in San Francisco but having lived abroad in her youth, she returned to the United States to exhibit her paintings with Marcel Duchamp and others at the 1917 Exhibition of the Society of Independent Artists in New York. Her friendship with Duchamp involved her in the most avant-garde art group of the time, which included Man Ray, Francis Picabia, Henry Miller, Anaïs Nin, and the Los Angeles–based collectors Louise and Walter Arensberg. Beato, as she was often called, moved to Southern California at about the

Above, left to right:
Harrison McIntosh, United States, b. 1914.

Vase, 1967. Stoneware with matte glaze.
H.: 15½ in. Promised gift of Catherine
McIntosh. TR.12733.

Large Platter, c. 1975. Stoneware with matte
glaze. Diam.: 15¼ in. Gift of Howard and
Gwen Laurie Smits. M.87.1.89.

same time as the Natzlers and lived much of her life associated with the Theosophical community in Ojai, California, founded in 1946 by Krishnamurti, Aldous Huxley, and Annie Besant.

Wood's marvelously kitschy drawings on slightly off-centered vessels and her colorful luster glazes set her apart from other potters since her first one-person exhibition at the America House Gallery in New York in 1949. Her intense wit is evident in her playful ceramics, although both she and her work had a more serious side. She made several trips to India for the United States Department of State, and she was a cherished figure in California in her saris and prodigious amounts of Indian silver folk jewelry. Her books about her eventful life and work are in most ceramists' libraries. She and her works won the respect of the new ceramic avant-garde that emerged in the fifties, and her off-kilter contribution to the Southern California clay scene continued to the day she died.

Above, left to right:
Harrison McIntosh, United States, b. 1914.

Vase, 1954. Stoneware. H.: 11 ⅞ in. Gift
of Catherine McIntosh. M.82.203.2.

Bowl, c. 1960s. Stoneware with matte glaze.
W.: 7 ⅜ in. Gift of Catherine McIntosh.
M.82.203.4.

Rupert Deese, United States, b. 1920.
Grey Bottle, 1980s. Stoneware. H.: 7 in.
Gift of Howard and Gwen Laurie Smits.
M.90.82.11.

Far from California but nevertheless an influence second to Leach and Hamada, Lucie Rie (1902–1995) from Austria and Hans Coper (1920–1981) from Germany, emigrated to England, where they met, in 1939. Coper initially assisted Rie in her pottery, although both artists developed unique formal statements: Rie's stark bowl forms and dramatic vases coated with soft mattes, manganese gold, and fine line decorations; Coper's bold pedestal shaped pots invoking Cycladic figures. Both mentored several generations of international clay workers but did not become well known and respected in the United States until several decades later; today their ceramic works are among the highest priced on the art market.

My own career in ceramics began when, as a painting major at Mills College in Oakland, California, I took a ceramics course from Carlton Ball my last semester, in 1946. In the summer of 1947 Ball, always interested in acquiring new technological skills, arranged a six-week workshop for Clarence Merrit, the glaze technologist from the New York State College of Ceramics at Alfred University, Alfred, New York, and invited me to attend. The workshop inspired me to apply to Alfred, the only ceramics college in the world.

Gertrud **Natzler,** Austria, active United
States; 1908–1971. **Otto Natzler,** Austria,
active United States, b. 1908.

Pilgrim Bottle (H252), 1956. Earthenware with
yellow crater glaze. H.: 17 in. Gift of Howard
and Gwen Laurie Smits. M.87.1.102.

Opposite, left:
Bowl (3819), 1943. Earthenware with gray lava
glaze with turquoise overflow. Diam.: 8½ in.
Gift of Rose A. Sperry 1972 Revocable Trust.
M.72.105.5.

Opposite, right:
Double-Curved Bottle (J276), 1957.
Earthenware with cherry-red glaze. H.: 22 in.
Gift of Howard and Gwen Laurie Smits.
M.87.1.103.

Beatrice Wood working on her wheel
in Ojai, California, 1992. Photograph
© Marlene Wallace, courtesy of Frank
Lloyd Gallery, Santa Monica, California.

Beatrice Wood, United States,
1893–1998. *Double Bottle,* c. 1970.
Earthenware. H.: 9⅔ in. Gift of Howard
and Gwen Laurie Smits. M.87.1.180.

Vivika Heino and Daniel Rhodes had earned the first MFA degrees offered at Alfred in 1940–41, but in those days the program emphasized low-fire ceramics. The chairman of ceramic design, Charles Harder, had spent the war years reading books about Asian ceramics and experimenting on his own with high-temperature Chinese reduction red, celadon, and hare's-fur glazes. By 1949, when I arrived, Alfred taught the gamut from low to high fire in all atmospheres.

I came to Los Angeles in 1950 with my degree in ceramic design and applied for jobs at Gladding, McBean and other potteries. But none of them employed designers, since most took their molds from other manufacturers' dinnerware forms. Eventually I found work for a few months at a small art pottery, Max Weil. Then, in spring 1951, Norma Friswold, who was teaching in the new ceramics department at Los Angeles City College on Vermont Boulevard, became ill and asked me to substitute for her. (I'd met Friswold at the Mills summer session in 1947; she was one of the students Laura Andreson had sent to learn throwing from Carlton Ball.)

Susan Harnly Peterson, United States, b. 1925. *Low Bowl (Homage to Opals),* 1998. Stoneware. Diam.: 12⁷/₈ in. Promised gift of Hannah and Russ Kully. TR.12765.

At City College Ken Price (b. 1935) and Billy Al Bengston (b. 1934), who would later become major figures in the California art scene, dropped in occasionally to work in clay, as they did later when I was teaching at Chouinard. I also met two astute secondary-school art supervisors in the Los Angeles city system, A. Kleihauer and Evangeline Heisig, who monitored my classes. They saw my work in stoneware and porcelain in the summer of 1951 at *5000 Years of Clay,* an exhibition curated by Richard Petterson and Millard Sheets (professors of ceramics and painting, respectively, at Scripps College). I believe mine were the first high-temperature, reduction-fired stoneware and porcelain pieces exhibited in this region.

The art supervisors mentioned me to Nelbert Chouinard, who directed the Chouinard Art Institute in downtown Los Angeles. Mrs. Chouinard had begun her school of fine arts in 1917 with, as she always said, "a war-widow's pension." It became famous in the United States for its excellent, well-recognized local and international faculty— Alexander Archipenko and Lyonel Feininger taught there—and its purist art curriculum, which led to a certificate rather than a degree. In June 1952 I arrived, at Mrs. Chouinard's bidding, to begin a ceramics department, primarily because she wanted something "more vocational" to offer veterans who had federal G.I. Bill funding for advanced education. She told me to build kilns that could be carried away by forklift in the middle of the night in case her creditors threw her out of the building at 8th Street and Grand View Avenue.

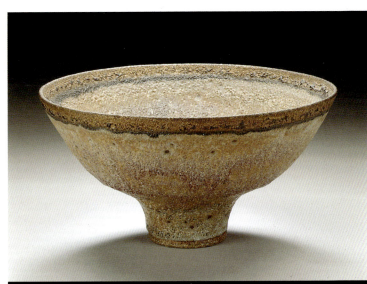

Lucie Rie, Austria, active England; 1902–1995.

Left:
Crater Bowl, 1982. Porcelain.
Diam.: 8½ in. Gift of Howard and Gwen Laurie Smits.
M.87.1.135.

Below, left:
Vase, 1979. Porcelain. H.: 7¼ in.
Gift of Howard and Gwen
Laurie Smits. M.87.1.132.

Hans Coper, Germany,
active England; 1920–1981.
Dog Bone, 1965. Stoneware.
H.: 8¾ in. Gift of Howard
and Gwen Laurie Smits.
M.87.1.29.

Lucie Rie, Austria, active
England; 1902–1995. *Tall Vase*
(two views), c. 1970. Porcelain.
H.: 12½ in. Gift of Howard and
Gwen Laurie Smits. M.87.1.137.

With Mike Kalan, a ceramics engineer and graduate of Alfred, whom I'd met through the American Ceramic Society, I designed an updraft twelve-burner open-fire (no muffle) gas kiln for high-temperature reduction. This kiln, really an ancient design, fired from the bottom with the atmosphere going up through the ware and out an open flue at the top, controlled by a damper. The burners were placed underneath the chassis, which was suspended above the floor on a frame (as opposed to the downdraft-style kiln built directly on the ground I had known at Alfred) so that a forklift could carry it over the back wall of the ceramic patio at Chouinard if necessary. I believe that this type of kiln—economical, capacious, and easy to fire in relatively short time—was ultimately responsible for the large scale for which West Coast ceramic art of the fifties and sixties became famous.

At Chouinard I created an Alfred-style curriculum that taught hand building, wheel throwing, plaster model carving (by hand and on a plaster wheel), mold making, slip casting, and jiggering, and I taught clay and glaze chemistry. John Mason (b. 1927)—today one of the most outstanding figures in contemporary international ceramics—walked into the studio when I was setting it up and asked if he could be my assistant in this new program; Mrs. Chouinard agreed. We began the courses in summer session 1952. All students worked in one big room, at different levels of experience, on a multitude of projects in every area of the ceramic vocabulary.

That December an outside influence entered the California pottery scene when I hosted Bernard Leach, Shōji Hamada, and Sōetsu Yanagi in a three-week workshop at Chouinard, with about thirty invited participants from around the country. (I'd met Leach during his first visit to United States, in 1949, when he'd worked with the Alfred graduate students.) The workshop was the culmination of their tour of U.S. art schools, universities, and ceramic alliances. Starting in New York, the men traveled to North Carolina, where they met Josef and Anni Albers, David Weinrib, Karen Karnes, and Robert Turner at the famous experimental Black Mountain College. In the West, they visited the culture that at the time they classified and lectured about as the "American taproot," Native American potters. Leach and Hamada believed that it was necessary to make pottery from a traditional wellspring like the root of a tree. It was years before they understood that the American potter's taproot was not Native American culture but all the world's societies from which the United States was born.

John Mason working in the ceramics studio at Chouinard Art Institute, c. 1953. Photograph courtesy of Susan Peterson.

Hamada had read of the work of the potter María Martínez many years earlier in Japan, and Leach, Hamada, and Yanagi were eager to come to this fountainhead. Leach describes the visit in my book *The Living Tradition of María Martínez* (Kodansha International, 1977), writing that on their arrival at the isolated pueblo in New Mexico where Martínez lived, they found no one about but suddenly spotted a wisp of black smoke rising in the air. The smoke led them to Martínez doing a bonfire smothered with horse manure to create carbon-deposition reduction for her famous black pots with matte-black designs. In Santa Fe they met the painter Georgia O'Keeffe and the designer Alexander Girard, who had an astonishing collection of folk art and ceramics. Hamada bought six Mimbres pots from Girard for his own enormous collection.

At Chouinard, Hamada made pots, Leach talked and made pots, and Yanagi lectured daily on folk arts of the world. Richard Petterson constructed a treadle wheel for Leach; for Hamada he built a stick-turned chestnut Chinese wheel with four holes on the top surface, the type Hamada used at home. Sitting in a lotus position, Hamada would insert a stick into one of the holes and spin the wheel several revolutions. This arduous design, which he refused to exchange for an easier type, required him to throw the pot in sections, upon which coils or other sections could be added and rethrown. He said this method helped him to achieve the crisp line changes he wanted in his forms. He approached clay intuitively. He once told me, "People use the words 'to create' very readily, but I don't like to use them very often. The things that I do, my wares, are not made but born. If you can't give birth to the thing then you can't call it creativity. But that is so difficult. Really, if you don't have some kind of help from God you can't give birth to things."

Shōji Hamada throwing pots outside Lang Gallery, Scripps College, Claremont, California, c. 1952. Photograph courtesy of Scripps College.

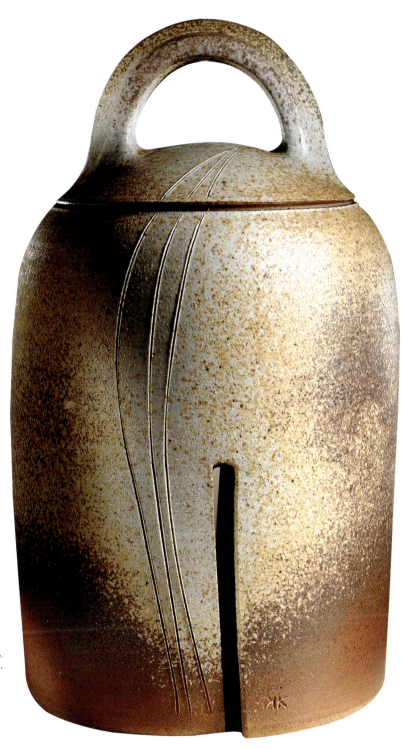

Karen Karnes, United States, b. 1925. *Vessel,* 1987. Stoneware, wheel thrown, glazed, and wood fired. H.: 16½ in. Gift of Howard and Gwen Laurie Smits. AC1995.194.1.1–.2. Detail opposite.

Robert Turner, United States, b. 1913.

Above, left:
De Chelly Vase, 1983. Stoneware. H.: 10 in.
Gift of Howard and Gwen Laurie Smits.
M.87.1.173.

Left:
Ife, 1997–99. White stoneware, porcelain-
glazed and sandblasted. H.: 12¾ in. Gift
of Rosalind Turner Zuses, courtesy of Helen
Drutt, Philadelphia. TR.12744.

Karen Karnes, United States, b. 1925.
Vessel, 1994. Stoneware, wood fired. W.: 21 in.
Smits Ceramics Purchase Fund. AC1999.48.1.

Ralph Bacerra, United States,
b. 1938. *Portrait Vessel,* 1994.
Whiteware. H.: 34½ in. Smits
Ceramics Purchase Fund.
AC1995.117.1.1–.2.

Recently the influence of Leach and Hamada on pottery in this country has been reeval-
uated in international exhibitions and magazine articles. Before their 1952 visit, U.S. potters
had little contact with Zen Buddhism, and few seemed to revere either folk art or the unknown
craftsperson. Zen is assumed to have had a major influence on West Coast ceramics in the
1950s. And yet, however much the work process we admired and valued shared qualities with
the Zen experience, I think that this was a coincidence. It was more by their example than
by their philosophies that Leach and Hamada inspired the resurgence in Asian, especially
Japanese and Korean, styles of vessel making that is still apparent in clay work today.

The education of ceramists blossomed in the fifties as California instituted a state college
system and constructed more university campuses. Schools were graduating overflowing
classes of potters and sculptors who in turn began new clay departments or did their own
work. In 1952 Glen Lukens took a leave of absence from the University of Southern California
and brought Vivika Heino (1910–1995) from New Hampshire as his replacement. Heino had
a degree from Alfred and had taken a Lukens class in Chautauqua, New York, at one of the
tented summer workshops that were popular at the time. Lukens's studio at USC was fitted
with wheels made by the use of a shaft and a round plaster bat in place of a sewing machine
on a treadle wheel. Lukens taught students to coil and trim with a carving tool on these
wheels. He had a glaze spray booth and a small kiln. Heino added a larger low-fire gas kiln
for the earthenware temperature she had learned at Alfred.

By then tool- and die maker Otto Heino (b. 1915) was also a potter,
having taken my course at Chouinard. Together Vivika and Otto went
on to become renowned studio potters, making dinnerware for famous
personalities and accessories for Hollywood movie sets, but always main-
taining a studio filled with pots, mostly thrown but some hand built, with
mostly, by now, high-fired reduction glazes. They made an exemplary
income, as they said, "only from pots."

Into this amazing potpourri of low- and high-fire clay, of whirlpools of burgeoning knowledge,
of bursting-at-the-seams growth in the California environment, dropped a young man from Montana
named Peter Voulkos (b. 1924). We had heard of him because he was winning prizes in juried
exhibitions for his classic, functional stoneware. When Millard Sheets became the director of the
newly reorganized Los Angeles County Art Institute (later renamed the Otis Art Institute) in 1954,
he invited the prizewinner Voulkos to join his new faculty and build a ceramics department.

Voulkos began with equipment similar to what I had installed across MacArthur Park at
Chouinard, but he and Mike Kalan built even larger kilns and used more powerful gear-reduction
variable-speed motors for potter's wheels. The move to California seemed to unleash a frenetic
spirit in Voulkos. He was unorthodox in everything he did, from combining arbitrary materials in
unmeasured amounts for clay bodies and glazes, to the macho way he maneuvered clay. Students
and friends congregated around Voulkos, especially at night. While we watched, sitting on orange
crates, he would throw what seemed like a hundred cylinders—round, oval, tall, short shapes—
and stack them wet on shelves like library books. When the clay stiffened, or even before, he would
begin the assembly of several mammoth sculptures. This was the best show in town. Fred Marer,
a mathematics professor at City College who was interested in ceramics, sat around making notes

and writing the first Voulkos publicity articles. There is no question that Voulkos began in the fifties to influence the whole world with his monumental work and his Pied Piper personality.

Vivika Heino resigned her USC position after three years in spring 1955, planning to return to New Hampshire, and I assumed a tenured professorship at the university in September. Mrs. Chouinard then hired Vivika to replace me at Chouinard. When after three more years Vivika finally did return to New Hampshire, Ralph Bacerra (b. 1938), her former student, took the job and taught legions more potters.

At USC I developed a unique undergraduate curriculum for the BFA major in ceramics, and we accepted about twenty graduate students each year for work toward the MFA. As at Chouinard, and following my Alfred training, I included mold making, slip casting, and jiggering for industrial ceramic design, installed a laboratory-size filter press for plastic porcelain bodies, and taught the chemistry of materials and mathematical glaze calculation as well as beginning through advanced levels of hand building, wheel throwing, and architectural ceramics. At the end of my first year, Dean Donald Goodall allowed me a second professor and I chose my former teacher Carlton Ball, who taught with me eleven years before moving to the College of Puget Sound. In 1972 I moved to Hunter College, City University of New York, to build a new ceramics department, where I spent the rest of my teaching career. Eventually John Mason joined me there until he retired.

In the following years the Otis, Chouinard, and USC groups—Voulkos and some of his first students, Paul Soldner (b. 1921), Henry Takemoto (b. 1930), Michael Frimkess (b. 1937), Jerry Rothman (b.1933), Mac McClain (b. 1923), and I and my students Mason and Price and a few others—moved in and out of each other's spheres. Each of us worked independently and experimented with new options of all sorts, throwing, hand building, cutting, and slashing clay into uncommon forms, often in the enormous scale made possible by our big kilns. A vital camaraderie and excitement permeated the group and the work.

Price, who graduated from USC in 1957, became one of the most innovative of all ceramic artists. He perfected engobes and glazes in the fifties and sixties and more recently has been coating fired clay surfaces with a combination of acrylics. Mason was one of the first ceramists in the contemporary world to develop large-scale hand-built techniques and continues to make difficult slab constructions of enormous size fired at high temperatures in reduction atmospheres. Solo shows at LACMA by Mason in 1966 and Price in 1978 were landmarks. These two

Otto Heino, United States, b. 1915. **Vivika Heino,** United States, 1910–1995. *Wood Ash Bottle #149,* 1994. Porcelain. H.: 12 in. Gift of Otto Heino in memory of Vivika Heino. AC1995.189.1

artists, along with Voulkos, Toshiko Takaezu (b. 1922), and Jun Kaneko (b. 1942), have been consistently exhibited in major international museums.

Other decorative arts influences intersected with and inspired innovations in ceramic art. LaGardo Tackett, an architect turned potter, created stark white unglazed lamps and tall floor vases for the interiors of houses that Gregory Ain, Raphael Soriano, Craig Ellwood, Richard Neutra, and A. Quincy Jones were designing. Charles Eames made wonderful plywood furniture and entertained Shōji Hamada when he came to town. Max and Rita Lawrence created a new market with an imaginative company, Architectural Ceramics, to manage and distribute landscape and public-space, mass-produced, but handmade works by potter David Cressy, a UCLA graduate. In Northern California Brian and Edith Heath mass-produced the first stoneware dinnerware and won the Museum of Modern Art Good Design Award. Malcolm Leland, another well-known Los Angeles potter, became a designer of slick interior accessories and sculptured building facades. George James designed for Hoffman Tile Corporation, Ontario, California, the first stoneware floor and wall tile ever produced in the United States. Several years later Millard Sheets headed a group, including Henry Takemoto, Dora DeLarios, Harrison McIntosh, and Jerry Rothman (b. 1933), that designed tile for Gladding, McBean. Thus a valid but different type of creativity was marching in tandem with the Voulkos-and-company miracle.

Record attendance at national and local juried exhibitions confirmed the rising interest in handmade objects in the fifties and sixties. The most important annual shows were the Ceramic National exhibition at the Everson Museum, Syracuse, New York, founded in 1932, and the Wichita National Decorative Art and Ceramic Exhibition, founded in 1945 by Maude Schollenberger, director of the Wichita Art Association Museum in Kansas. For about forty years, until they ceased in the early 1970s, both competitions brought hundreds of objects to public attention. The California Design Exhibition, founded by the Pasadena Art Museum in 1954 and expanded in 1962 for several more years by director Eudorah Moore, was symbolic of the tremendous influence of handcraft and manufactured craft in the state.

In the Midwest and the eastern states, the West Coast ceramics movement was regarded with awe and disbelief and took hold as an influence only gradually. Daniel Rhodes (1911–1989), an Alfred graduate who had returned to his alma mater to teach in 1948, came to the first American Craft Council's national conference in 1957 at Asilomar, near Monterey, California. He saw the exhibition of California's large pots and ceramic sculpture and asked me how many pieces were luted together, for instance, in Ball's five-foot-tall vase with its classic Greek-inspired form, celadon glazed and decorated with wax and iron. When I told him that Ball

Susan Peterson and Carlton Ball, professors at the University of Southern California Ceramic Art Department, 1957. Photograph courtesy of Susan Peterson.

had thrown it in one piece, Rhodes couldn't fathom how. He hadn't seen the powerful variable-speed wheels and big kilns that we had in Southern California, and he never did install them at Alfred or experiment with larger-scale ceramics himself. In fact, what was going on in the West seemed not to affect any of the potters from the East who attended the remarkable gathering at Asilomar. Even afterward, the western developments and the artists who were making them were still separate from the easterners.

One who did understand, at least philosophically, was the legendary Aileen Osborne Vanderbilt Webb, who founded the American Craft Council in New York in 1945 and became the prime espouser of the validity of handcraft in an industrialized society. Mrs. Webb also founded the School for American Craftsmen, now at the Rochester Institute of Technology; America House, a sales outlet in Manhattan; the Museum of Contemporary Craft (now the Museum of American Craft) in New York; the magazine *Craft Horizons* (now *American Craft*); and the World Craft Council, a division of UNESCO founded in 1964. Regional organizations still exist around the world as a result of her efforts, and the market for ceramics would not be what it is today without her. Through *Craft Horizons,* the magazine edited for more than twenty years by the indomitable Rose Slivka, who was the first to write about the ceramics explosion in Southern California, and through the exhibitions at America House, the West was at least introduced to the East.

Meanwhile, in the Midwest, ceramic artists evolved independently of the western movement or the Alfred idiom. Maija Grotell (1899–1978) from Finland, who began a ceramics department at Cranbrook Art Institute, Bloomfield Hills, Michigan, in 1938, pioneered glazing techniques, including using mothballs to reduce copper to a red color in an oxidizing electric kiln, and gave many well-known clay artists of today their start. Sheldon Carey, at the University of Kansas, developed glazes from local volcanic ash; Harding Black at San Antonio was an expert thrower; Charles Lakofsky and Viktor Schreckengost made vessels and satirical ceramic sculptures in Ohio. But as the art critic Lucy Lippard has said, the ceramics on the West Coast became known as art, while the ceramics of the East Coast were still crafts.

Voulkos moved to the University of California at Berkeley in 1959 to begin a ceramics department. The new group that formed around him there included Jim Melchert (b. 1930), Ron Nagle (b. 1939), Richard Shaw (b. 1941), Viola Frey (b. 1933), and Marilyn Levine (b. 1935). (Works by these artists are illustrated in the essay by Peter Selz herein, p. 159.) As Nagle recalled in an interview with Michael McTwigan in the catalogue for his retrospective in Oakland in 1993, when he first saw slides of work by the various Voulkos colleagues in Southern California, "That was it, nothing else mattered. I had never seen anything like it in my life. . . . and seeing all that goofy stuff that was so inventive . . . it just took my breath away." While influenced by Voulkos, each of these artists maintained a personal style. But Voulkos was the original phenomenon, and I believe he will take his place in art history among the American greats such as Willem de Kooning and Jackson Pollock.

Jun Kaneko, Japan, b. 1942. *Dango,* 1993. Ceramic, glazed. H.: 27 in. Promised gift of Lynn and Jerry Myers. TR.12732.11.

Toshiko Takaezu, United States
(Hawaii), b. 1922. *Homage to Ko'olau
Range,* 1994–95. Stoneware, glazed.
H.: 57 in. Gift of Karen Johnson Boyd.
TR.12688. Detail on p. 85.

Maija Grotell, Finland, 1899–1978. *Vase,*
c. 1947. Stoneware. H.: 12½ in. Smits
Ceramics Purchase Fund. M.91.167.1.

Anthony Prieto, Spain, active United States;
1913–1967. *Vessel,* 1961. Earthenware. H.: 14¾ in.
Smits Ceramics Purchase Fund. M.90.128.

The gifted Robert Arneson (1930–1992), who graduated from the program run by Anthony
Prieto (1913–1967) at Mills College in 1958, went to teach at the University of California at Davis
in 1962, and a group of his followers became leaders—Robert Brady (b. 1946) and David Gilhooly
(b. 1943) to name two. Arneson was unique in his approach to satirical art, whether dealing with
an object such as a typewriter or a human head that might or might not be a self-portrait. Jun
Kaneko, a painter and a potter, arrived in Los Angeles from Japan in 1963, worked in Jerry Rothman's
dinnerware pottery, built kilns in people's backyards, and became the focus of another group of
young artists. Kaneko revamped several college ceramic departments before leaving to build his
ceramic *dangos* (named after Japanese dumplings, which they resemble), both in large and small
scale, in the brick kiln at Bemis Foundation in Omaha, Nebraska, and to demonstrate and exhibit
elsewhere in the world. It is an axiom that clay people are gregarious and adventurous.

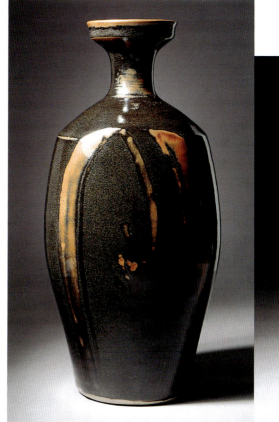

David Leach, England, b. 1911.
Temoku Bottle, 1972. Stoneware.
H.: 14 in. Gift of Howard and
Gwen Laurie Smits. M.87.1.73.

Janet Leach, United States, active
England; 1918–1997. *Bottle,* 1970s.
Earthenware. H.: 9¾ in. Gift of Howard
and Gwen Laurie Smits. M.87.1.74.

Other groups arose around Toshiko Takaezu (b. 1922), a student of Maija Grotell (1899–1978), who taught at Cleveland Art Institute and Princeton; Robert Sperry (1927–1998), who had worked with Voulkos at Berkeley and with Patti Warashina (b. 1940) at the University of Washington; Ken Ferguson (b. 1928), an Alfred graduate, who reigned at Kansas City Art Institute until his retirement; and Rudy Autio (b. 1926) at the University of Montana. Bernard Leach was still Europe's foremost potter, and his followers, such as Warren Mackenzie (b. 1924), adhered to the ideals of mingei. Leach married the American potter Janet Darnell (1918–1997), who helped him continue his St. Ives pottery until his death in 1979. Leach's son David (b. 1911) is also a potter. Hamada, the national treasure of folk art in Japan, exerted such powerful influence in his lifetime that long after his death in 1978 Japanese ceramists are just beginning to find their own ways.

Ken Ferguson, United States, b. 1928.

Left:
Jar, 1996. Stoneware. H.: 24½ in. Promised gift
of Lynn and Jerry Myers. TR.12732.7.1–.2.

Above:
Rabbit Vessel, 1989. Stoneware. W.: 16½ in. Gift
of Howard and Gwen Laurie Smits in honor
of LACMA's twenty-fifth anniversary.
M.90.82.13.

Jeff Oestreich, United States, b. 1947. *Ewer and Beaked Pitcher,* 1999. Ceramic, wood- and salt-fired. Ewer h.: 5 1/2 in. Pitcher h.: 6 3/4 in. Promised gift of Ferrin Gallery. TR.12676.1.1–.2.

Warren Mackenzie, United States, b. 1924.

Left:
Tall Vase with Bosses, 1988. Stoneware. H.: 14¼ in. Gift of Howard and Gwen Laurie Smits in honor of LACMA's twenty-fifth anniversary. M.90.82.35.

Below:
Five-Sided Covered Bowl, 1989. Stoneware. H.: 5 in. Gift of Howard and Gwen Laurie Smits in honor of LACMA's twenty-fifth anniversary. M.90.82.36a–b.

John Parker Glick, United States, b. 1938. *Lidded Box with Feet,* 1996. Stoneware, soda-fired. W.: 16 in. Smits Ceramics Purchase Fund. AC1998.7.1.1–.2.

Randy Johnston, United States, b. 1950. *Stacked Box Form,* 1998. Ceramic, wood- and salt-fired. H.: 9⅞ in. Promised gift of Ferrin Gallery. TR.12674.1.1–.4

Michael Simon, United States, b. 1947. *Persian Jar with Birds,* 1998. Ceramic, wood- and salt-fired. H.: 6 in. Promised gift of Ferrin Gallery. TR.12678.1.1-.2

Other developments were outgrowths of the Scandinavian design movement of the thirties—cresting in the fifties—exemplified by Kai Frank and Kaliki Salmenhara in Finland; Natalie Krebs and Christian Poulson in Denmark; and Wilhelm Köge, Stig Lindberg, Karin Bjorquist, and Lisa Larsen in Sweden. Their works, which hark back to the Bauhaus principles of simple functional forms endowed with beauty, are still important statements in contemporary ceramic art. The painter Joan Miró, who worked with the potter Llorens Artigas, became known for extraordinary scale and inventive use of textured clay bodies and colorful surfaces, while Picasso continued a substantial clay oeuvre, begun in the thirties, of figures and paintings on platters. The British potter Michael Cardew (1901–1983) lived for thirty years in Abuja, Nigeria, influencing the art there. American painters and sculptors such as David Smith, Isamu Noguchi, and Louise Nevelson, excited by the flexibility and spontaneity possible with clay, used the medium for quick sketch and serious study. These and other important artists working internationally in clay were known to one another, visited one another, and developed independent approaches that influence and enrich the work of contemporary ceramists.

Michael Cardew, England, 1901–1983.

Above, left:
Large Plate, 1970. Stoneware, wheel thrown, with sgraffito decoration. Diam.: 16 in. Gift of Howard and Gwen Laurie Smits. M.87.1.22.

Above, right:
Tea Pot, 1960s. Earthenware. H.: 8 in. Gift of Betty Asher in honor of LACMA's twenty-fifth anniversary. M.91.122a–b.

The remarkable confluence of ideas, verve, and downright genius that sparked the ceramics explosion at the mid-twentieth century and beyond was due to a few stars who led the pack. Nearly all of these artists are still working, or their pieces survive in museums, in galleries, in the houses of collectors, and on the secondary market. Fifty years ago we could not have imagined the reverence in which these clay works are held today, but the fun of being in the vortex of exploration and development remains with those of us who were there. The original burst of energy has subsided into a public acceptance of ceramic art, as if it had always been this way. I hope that historians will continue giving credit to clay as art, and artists will continue to use this earthen material in invigorating new ways, or in transformations of the venerable old ways.

Susan Peterson is the author of *Pottery by American Indian Women: The Legacy of Generations; Shōji Hamada: A Potter's Way and Work; The Living Tradition of María Martínez;* and *The Craft and Art of Clay,* among other publications. A graduate of Mills College, California, and the New York State College of Ceramics at Alfred University, she has established ceramics departments at schools across the country, including Chouinard Art Institute, the University of Southern California, and Hunter College at the City University of New York.

Peter Voulkos, United States, b. 1924.
Standing Jar, 1954–56. Stoneware.
H.: 22½ in. Gift of Howard and Gwen
Laurie Smits in honor of LACMA's
twenty-fifth anniversary. M.90.82.55.

Paul Soldner, United States,
b. 1921. *Pedestal Piece 87–6,* 1987.
Clay, wheel thrown and altered,
salt vapored. H.: 28¼ in. Promised
gift of Lynn and Jerry Myers.
TR.12732.18.

Otis and Berkeley

Crucibles of the American Clay Revolution

GARTH
CLARK

During the twentieth century, there have been two primary approaches to ceramics. Advocates of the first, which is rooted in the late-nineteenth-century Arts and Crafts movement, create and admire finely crafted, decorative vessels in traditional shapes. The second approach emerged after World War II, when a small group of innovators sought to position their abstract, nonfunctional clay forms as high art. The extent to which the art/crafts distinction transfixes the ceramics world often bemuses newcomers. From the start, the crafts camp accused the art movement of poor handiwork, pretentiousness, and obsession with status; the artists, in turn, described the crafts approach as regressive and puritanical. The line between the groups is ill defined and blurry: Many leading ceramic artists started as craftspeople, and works made for decoration or use are collected as art. Nonetheless, the question of where ceramics belongs in the arts and crafts hierarchy still obsesses artists, curators, collectors, and dealers in the field.

The art ceramics movement began primarily on the West Coast. Between 1950 and 1980, California artists shattered traditional views of what clay art could and should be, introduced an original American aesthetic, and set the pace for the field in the United States and abroad. Variously titled the New Clay movement, the California Clay Rush, and the West Coast Ceramics Revolution, this trend was actually made up of at least four separate stylistic approaches, each incorporating wide diversity.

Peter Voulkos (b. 1924) and his students in Los Angeles in the mid-1950s ignited the fiery revolution that reinvented the humble pot as an object of contemporary aesthetic significance and also opened the door to ambitious sculptural expressions. Robert Arneson (1930–1992) was the father (though he often denied this paternity) of the figurative Funk movement that emerged in the California Bay Area in the early 1960s. Soon thereafter, a populist, high-process approach concerned with craft and the use of trompe l'oeil surfaces, which I have dubbed the "Super-Object," developed more or less simultaneously in Seattle (Fred Bauer, Howard Kottler, Patti Warashina), the Bay Area (Richard Shaw, Marilyn Levine), and Los Angeles (David Furman, Ed Ford).[1] Finally, there were the L.A. Chouinard School students (Ralph Bacerra, Adrian Saxe, Elsa Rady, Mineo Mizuno, Peter Shire, and others) who led the charge in the late 1970s for a distinctive postmodern style. They embraced many of the taboos of high art: pattern, decoration, the extravagance of court porcelains, and other influences rejected by modernist orthodoxy. Their work was colorful, smart, informed, refined to the point of slickness, with an urbane quality entirely different from the tone of Voulkos's or Arneson's work.

Collectively this is a formidable legacy of innovation, spanning two generations. No other group of artists in the United States comes close to matching the influence of West Coast ceramists on the character of American ceramic art today. Certainly without the work of Voulkos and his students in Los Angeles and then in Berkeley from 1950 to 1966, ceramics would occupy a different place in the art world today. This essay revisits that initial California clay revolution, evaluating its causes and impact and questioning some of its myths.

Elsa Rady, United States, b. 1943. *Winged Victory,* 1983. Porcelain, wheel thrown and glazed. W.: 14½ in. Gift of Howard and Gwen Laurie Smits. M.87.1.129.

Opposite:
Howard Kottler, United States, 1930–1989. *Blue Balls,* 1986. Earthenware. H.: 23 in. Gift of the Estate of Howard Kottler. AC1992.244.2.

Ralph Bacerra, United States, b. 1938.
Untitled Animal, 1976. Stoneware. W.: 39 in.
Promised gift of Lynn and Jerry Myers.
TR 12732.3.

According to conventional wisdom, the revolution began in 1954 in Los Angeles, when Millard Sheets, director of the Otis Art Institute (at that time officially named the Los Angeles County Art Institute but known as Otis), appointed Voulkos to set up the school's first ceramics department. In fact, the movement's roots extend nearly a decade earlier, to 1946, when the G.I. Bill was enacted to provide World War II ex-servicemen with a government-sponsored college education.

Many of the servicemen would never otherwise have considered college, and a surprising number chose to study art, perhaps as an antidote to the harsh experience of war. One of these was a twenty-two-year-old, recently discharged nose gunner from the U.S. Army Air Corps by the name of Peter Voulkos, who entered Montana State University to study painting. (Previously he had assumed that he would enter the family dry-cleaning business.) Indeed, so many returning servicemen enrolled for studio arts courses (including two future students of Voulkos, Mac McClain and Paul Soldner) that they jump-started a surge in university art education that continued into the 1970s, encouraging the formation of art departments, galleries, art museums, and arts groups. Aside from the raw talent of America's artists themselves, the G.I. Bill was the decisive catalyst in establishing America's dominant position in contemporary art.

Voulkos came to clay reluctantly. In his junior year he had to take ceramics to satisfy a requirement. As a budding painter he resented this detour but dutifully arrived for his first class with potter Frances Senska. He left a convert. His rapport with clay was immediate and intuitive. He had a precocious talent for working on the wheel and was soon making remarkably mature work: sturdy, soundly thrown forms with swirling wax-resist decoration and primitive stick drawings. In 1950, while still a student, he won his first national award, the Potters Association Prize at the fifteenth Ceramic National exhibition (America's premier ceramics showcase) at the Syracuse Museum of Fine Arts, Syracuse, New York (now the Everson Museum of Art). After completing a master's degree in ceramics and sculpture at the California College of Arts and Crafts in Oakland (1951–52), he became artist-in-residence with fellow Montana ceramist Rudy Autio (b. 1926) at the Archie Bray Foundation in Helena, Montana.

Group of three pots for which Peter Voulkos won the United States Potters Association Purchase Prize at the fifteenth Ceramic National at Syracuse Museum of Fine Art (now Everson Museum of Art) in 1950. Pots on left and right: collection of the Everson Museum. Middle vase: private collection. Photograph courtesy of the American Craft Council.

Shōji Hamada demonstrating at the wheel at the
Archie Bray Foundation, Helena, Montana, 1953.
Peter Voulkos observes closely from the bench.
Photograph courtesy of Garth Clark Gallery.

Above:
Bernard Leach instructing
students at the Archie Bray
Foundation, Helena, Montana,
1953. Photograph courtesy of
Garth Clark Gallery.

Top, right:
Peter Voulkos, United States,
b. 1924. *Tea Bowl,* 1953. H.: 4¼ in.
Stoneware, wheel thrown and
glazed. LACMA, gift of Howard
and Gwen Laurie Smits.
M.87.1.174.

It was there, in 1952, that he met the scholar-potter Bernard
Leach (1887–1979), then the most respected and influential
ceramist in the West. The Bray Foundation was a stop on Leach's
legendary United States lecture tour with potter Shōji Hamada
(1894–1978) and the crafts philosopher Sōetsu Yanagi, one of the
founders of the *mingei* movement. Voulkos found Leach and
Yanagi intellectually impressive, but it was Hamada's intuitive
touch with clay that moved him as an artist. Immediately after
the trio left Montana, Voulkos made a series of tea bowls
painted in the Japanese style in homage to Hamada.[2]

It is worth pausing for a moment to examine Leach and
his role in the field of ceramics. A gifted polymath, Leach was
raised in the Far East and educated at the Slade School of Art
in London. He then went to Japan to teach etching. There, at a
raku party for artists, actors, and poets (the entertainment was
decorating and glazing prefired pots that were then refired in
a raku kiln), he fell in love with the art of ceramics. In turn the
Japanese developed an enduring affection for this tweed-jack-
eted enthusiast of their culture.[3]

Leach remains the most influential potter of the century, not for his art, which was a touch regressive, but for his teaching and writing, and for the hold he had for decades on the intellectual heart of ceramics. By the time Voulkos met him, Leach's *A Potter's Book* had already been in print for many years. First published in 1940 and referred to as the Bible, it is now in its sixteenth edition, has never been out of print, and has sold more than 130,000 copies.

Leach persuasively argued the case for what Oliver Watson, curator of ceramics at London's Victoria and Albert Museum, defines as the "ethical" pot, rooted in function and the crafts.[4] The very name implies a moral authority based on a belief in the honesty and virtue of utility. Leach held that potters needed to know their place at the visual arts table, as creators of humble, useful vessels for ordinary people, and he attacked those potters "working by hand to please ourselves as artists first, and therefore producing only limited and expensive pieces...supported by collectors, purists, 'cranks' or 'arty' people rather than by the normal man or woman."[5] From his various visits to the United States Leach decided that ceramics in America had promise but also a potentially fatal shortcoming in that it "lacked a ceramic taproot" or indigenous tradition (outside of Native American pottery).[6]

Rudy Autio, United States, b. 1926. *Salt Creek Games,* 1984. Stoneware. H.: 14½ in. Gift of Howard and Gwen Laurie Smits. M.87.1.10.

When they met, Voulkos was making relatively conventional wares more or less in keeping with Leach's ideals. It could not have been apparent to either of them that Voulkos was only a few years away from the aesthetic breakthroughs that would free American ceramics from the traditional views that Leach sought to impose. For Voulkos and those who followed him, the lack of a taproot was actually a blessing, allowing them to invent new traditions or find contemporary freedoms with old ones. In Britain and Japan, on the other hand, the huge weight of historical achievement in ceramics tended to inhibit rather than liberate the contemporary artist.

Otis

By the time Voulkos arrived in Los Angeles in 1954, he had acquired some art-world sophistication. A workshop at Black Mountain College near Asheville, North Carolina, in 1953, had introduced him to several of the emerging forces in American art, Robert Rauschenberg, John Cage, and Merce Cunningham among them. After the workshop, M. C. Richards, the potter-poet, took Voulkos to New York, where he hung out at the infamous Cedar Bar on Tenth Street and met Franz Kline, Phillip Guston, and other "action painters" from the New York School (It was not until after his second visit with the group in 1958, however, that influence from their painting appeared in his art). He had already won awards for his vessels, which were powerful without being radical, distinctive without being too original, informed without being academic. Millard Sheets, head of the Otis Art Institute, greatly admired these handsome pots and bought several for his own collection. Influenced by the thin-necked bottles of Mill Valley potter Anthony Prieto, the rich palette of Scandinavian stoneware potters Carl-Harry Stålhane and Stig Lindberg, and the calligraphic painting on Japanese tea bowls, they were lively, eclectic objects but still the kind of pots you could safely take home to mother.

Above:
The ceramics studio, Otis, 1955–56. The tall vessels are by Paul Soldner; the pots on the tables and the shelves are by Peter Voulkos and his students. Photograph courtesy of Paul Soldner.

Right:
Henry Takemoto, Peter Voulkos, and Jerry Rothman at Otis, 1957. Photograph courtesy of Garth Clark Gallery.

Voulkos had arrived in California at a perfect moment. When he was setting up his department, the San Francisco renaissance was already under way. Jack Kerouac's *On the Road* and Allen Ginsberg's *Howl* were about to be published. Coffee bars sprang up in San Francisco and Los Angeles, filled with soulful poets and free-spirited musicians. Miles Davis and the Modern Jazz Quartet were all the rage, folk music was taking hold, and drugs, particularly hallucinogens, were being promoted as the route to new levels of awareness. California was the center of a growing fascination with Eastern philosophy, and the books and teachings of Allan Watts popularized Zen Buddhism. The whole culture was wide open to aesthetic change and radicalism; as Suzanne Foley comments in her catalogue essay for the 1981 Whitney Museum exhibition *Ceramic Sculpture: Six Artists,* "Physically and psychically removed from the New York art world, a California artist felt little restrained by the East Coast's hierarchal and traditional definitions of fine art."[7] To become a player in this era of free experiment, ceramics needed a guide with the vision and courage to lead the way. It found one in Voulkos.

Beatrice Wood, United States, 1893–1998. *Gold Lustre Bottle,* c. 1960. Earthenware, glazed. H.: 7½ in. Gift of Stanley and Betty Sheinbaum. AC1998.244.7.

Voulkos's initial response to the local clay scene, however, was less than enthusiastic. Southern California had a lively commercial ceramics tradition and was one of the leading centers for dinnerware production in the United States, but studio ceramics in this region was still young. There was no regional Native American tradition, and the Arts and Crafts movement, except for a few minor potteries, had bypassed L.A. ceramics. Not until 1938, when Glen Lukens organized the First All Californian Ceramic Exhibition, had the small, scattered group of studio potters come together into a community, and throwing on the wheel had not been generally introduced until the late 1940s.

In the mid-1950s, California studio potters were still working in a prewar aesthetic. (See the essay by Susan Peterson herein, p. 87, for more about these potters' work.) The Viennese émigrés Gertrud and Otto Natzler made exquisite, refined pots, as did Harrison McIntosh (who taught for Voulkos at Otis). But most of this work had become too precious, conservative, and decorative for Voulkos's tastes. He considered the Dada veteran Beatrice Wood the only real artist working in clay, but as much as he liked her wobbly lustre pots, they did not inspire him. The many ceramics classes and programs that had developed since the war (Laura Andreson taught at the University of California, Los Angeles, and Susan Peterson and Vivika Heino at the Chouinard Art Institute) focused on functional, well-crafted vessels, which Voulkos had already mastered. He was impatient to plunge into a more expressive realm.

The L.A. art scene was just beginning to percolate, and Voulkos enjoyed an easy rapport with this adventurous young community that included Ed Keinholz, Robert Irwin, and Craig Kauffman. They admired his energy and expressive power, the oddly misshapen pots that tumbled out of the studio, and the ambitious scale (in tonnage of clay) of the Otis experiment. Both Irwin and Kauffman titled paintings *Black Raku* in recognition of the work of Otis students.

Word of Voulkos's arrival quickly spread among local potters. Thirty years old, charismatic, handsome, gregarious, and possessed of a seemingly bottomless well of energy, he attracted a stellar and unconventional group of students. Paul Soldner (b. 1921) was the first to join in 1954, followed in 1955 by John Mason (b. 1927), who had already studied ceramics for four years at Chouinard, and Mac McClain (b. 1923). In 1956 Billy Al Bengston (b. 1934) enrolled, and Michael Frimkess (b. 1937), who had been admitted to the Institute at age fifteen, decided to major in ceramics. Ken Price (b. 1935), also from Chouinard, entered the program in spring 1957, followed in the fall by Henry Takemoto (b. 1930) and Jerry Rothman (b. 1933).

Although there were women students, such as Janice Roosevelt and Carol Radcliffe, for the most part Otis's pot shop was a supermacho environment. California in the 1950s and 1960s was surprisingly unsympathetic to women ceramists. Vivika Heino, Laura Andreson, and Susan Peterson earned respect as educators, but men dominated the emerging art field. It was not until the early 1970s that local women ceramists—early notables included Viola Frey and Karen Breschi— began to receive attention. Meanwhile, on the East Coast and in the Midwest during the 1950s and 1960s, Karen Karnes, Toshiko Takaezu, Ruth Duckworth, Margaret Israel, Betty Woodman, and many others established themselves as both teachers and makers.

Voulkos was an unconventional teacher. There was no curriculum, so students needed self-motivation. Almost every other ceramics course in the country focused on training teachers, but Voulkos was determined to produce working artists. About the same age as his students, he replaced the pedagogic role with a collaborative spirit. As Mac McClain later recalled, "It became quickly evident that all of us would be sharing a studio with each involved at their own independent level. Pete radiated an overwhelming individuality, a relaxed and humorous charm, radical creative initiative, and an enjoyable mix of down-home earthiness and aesthetic brilliance. We were all roughly the same age, part of the post–World War II generation of young artists searching for a place to make things."[8]

Paul Soldner, United States,
b. 1921. *Vase,* late 1960s.
Earthenware. H.: 15½ in. Gift of
Daniel Ostroff. AC1992.293.1.

The serious work was done at night, partly because it suited Voulkos's night-owl temperament and partly because some students had day jobs (John Mason, for instance, worked as a dinnerware designer). The core students would meet late in the day and work into the early morning hours. At times the group would produce hundreds of pieces in a week, many of which would be destroyed in editing or lost in the kiln. Part of the ritual was gathering for breakfast after 2 a.m. There was a palpable excitement in the air, the feeling of being on the edge of a real discovery. As Voulkos remembers, "Everything started falling into place, [and] I could see what I had to do."[9]

Initially the accent at Otis was on the vessel and the wheel. The 4,000-year-old invention that harnessed the power of centrifugal force was the energy source and vital center (literally and figuratively) of the Otis experiment. In 1956 Voulkos spoke about this dynamic with Conrad Brown:

"When you are experimenting on the wheel there are a lot of things you can not explain. You just say to yourself, 'the form will find its way'—it always does.... That's what makes it exciting. The minute you begin to feel you understand what you're doing it loses that searching quality.... You finally reach a point where you are no longer concerned with keeping this blob of clay centered on the wheel and up in the air. Your emotions take over and what happens just happens.... Pottery has to be more than an exercise in facility—the human element, expression, is usually badly neglected."[10]

Peter Voulkos throwing pottery on potter's kick wheel at Otis, c. 1955. Photograph courtesy of Peter Voulkos.

Rare film footage shot at the Archie Bray Foundation around 1953 shows a young Voulkos throwing pots, an act of such sensual intimacy that the viewer feels a touch of voyeuristic discomfort, seeing the artist fondle, manipulate, and coax his vessels into life.

Voulkos emphatically rejected the golden rule of throwing that teachers drummed into their students: that a pot must have "lift and life," a visual lightness, an upward line from foot to belly. Voulkos countered with "dump and death,"[11] welcoming clay's slumping and earth-bound quality. By 1955–56 he and his students had turned from conventional, symmetrical vessels to muscular, distorted, torn, cut, and reshaped pots. McClain, Voulkos, and Mason created bottle-shaped forms that were almost solid chunks of clay.

In a 1966 dialogue with Voulkos, Soldner remembered the actual moment of breakthrough, when the Otis aesthetic emerged:

"Do you remember when, probably for the first time, you broke with the symmetry of the bottle? Some good-looking girls came in from Chouinard Art School and asked if you would throw a big pot for them. You threw the pot, and they were impressed. . . . I remember you kept looking at the pot. . . . And after they left you went over and cut the top off. Then you threw four or five spouts and started sticking them around the rim. And that didn't seem to work, because it was still the same old bottle lip. Then you pared that off. The pot was still soft. Then you recentered it on the wheel and gouged three huge definitions—the top third, the center third and the bottom third. In one afternoon you went from one kind of thinking to something completely different."[12]

But contrary to what has so often been written,[13] the Otis group did not reject ceramics traditions—only the narrow, restrictive tastes in Western pottery to which most American potters had previously subscribed. Indeed, Voulkos was fascinated by the rich history of ceramics and deeply curious about where he and his group belonged in the millennia-long canons of the art. He was an obsessive browser of books and magazine articles, and he took his students on a journey through the history of ceramics that, although haphazard and without concern for chronological or cultural borders, awakened in them a respect and passion for its legacy.

The greatest influence on Voulkos during his first two years at Otis was the ceramic art of Pablo Picasso. Voulkos was enthralled by the kinetic energy between painted surface and form in these pots, the way Picasso manipulated and restructured the appearance of the form, flattening, foreshortening, distorting, and relocating the central focus with a stroke of his brush. Picasso had discovered the complex choreography between painted line and three-dimensional form, an epiphany he described in a conversation with Henri Laurens: "You ought to go into ceramics! I made a head. . . . It is amazing. Well, you can look at it from all angles, and it is flat. Of course it is the painting that makes it flat. I also did something else: I painted on rounded surfaces. I painted balls. It is surprising . . . it escapes you: it turns around the ball."[14]

Seated Warrior, Japan, sixteenth century.
Haniwa figure in terra-cotta. H.: 43 in.
LACMA, Mr. and Mrs. Allan C. Balch Fund.
M.58.9.4.

Bizen Storage Jar, Japan, 1568–1615.
Stoneware. H.: 10⅜ in. LACMA, gift of the
family of Benjamin Johnson in his memory.
M.91.249.

Picasso broke with centuries of passive emblematic decoration in Western ceramics, wherein the actual physical boundaries of the form determined the parameters of decoration. Voulkos later explained what Picasso had taught him: "I brush on color to violate the form and it comes out a complete new thing which involves a painting concept on a three-dimensional surface, a new idea. These things are exploding, jumping off. I wanted to pick up that energy. That's different from decorating. Decorating enhances form, heightens the surface. I wanted to change the form, get more excitement going."[15]

Japanese ceramics provided another central, enduring influence, not only on the Otis group; potters throughout the United States, led by the evangelical zeal of Leach and his American students Alix and Warren Mackenzie, were turning to Japan for inspiration. Voulkos and his students particularly admired the earthy and rustic aesthetics of prehistoric, architectonic Haniwa sculpture, the subtle asymmetry of sixteenth-century black raku teabowls, and the pitted, burnt surfaces of seventeenth-century Shigaraki and Bizen ware. They also enjoyed the work of contemporary Japanese potters Kanjirō Kawai, Shōji Hamada, Toyo Kaneshige, and Kitaoji Rosanjin (the latter three visited California in the 1950s). Vivika Heino recalls a discernible change in Voulkos's work after he saw Rosanjin's exhibition in a Los Angeles gallery.[16] Voulkos also took his students to see Japanese Mingei pottery in Little Tokyo.[17]

Most Western potters saw the ideal of Japanese pottery as a destination to be reached through sincere imitation. The Otis group saw it more as a springboard. Much of the painting on their pots before 1958, which writers have ascribed to the influence of Abstract Expressionism, was actually derived from centuries-old calligraphic Japanese pottery decoration. The celebration of happenstance in the rugged wares of Shigaraki and Bizen gave the Otis group license to make cracks, warpage, crawling, and kiln accidents part of their syntax, in the process overturning the stultifying search for flawless form that had dominated the Western ceramics sensibility.

The Otis work was often far more furiously gestural and spontaneous than Japanese pottery. The group did not realize that in Japanese pottery spontaneity is actually achieved over a long period of time through an arduous process of control and growth, rather than at midnight in a moment of epiphany during a caffeine and nicotine adrenaline rush, and that Japanese happenstance is a matter of years of careful planning, precise kiln placement, and deliberate coaxing. These misunderstandings helped abstract the influences and give the Otis work its unique spirit and integrity.

Voulkos, a jazz addict, also studied classical flamenco guitar. Along with Price, who played piano, and Frimkess, who played saxophone, he frequented the L.A. jazz clubs and played music throughout the night in the ceramics studio. Soon he began to replace the simple, unified harmony of his early work with syncopation, dissonance, free-form structure, and playful extemporizing. As Price remarked, drawing an analogy between Voulkos's ceramic skills and music, "Technically, Voulkos was a master like Charlie Parker, who could play in any key."[18] Without torturing the metaphor, it is reasonable to say that as a group they worked much like a jazz ensemble—playing spontaneous, improvisational clay "riffs" on the wheel for hour after hour, responding to each other's energies, rhythms, and ideas.

Painting and sculpture, particularly by European artists, were also incorporated into the inspirational mix. Matisse's paper cutouts had an impact, as did the collages of Conrad Marca-Relli. Within hours of seeing Marca-Relli's exhibition at the Los Angeles County Museum of Art, Voulkos translated the painter's use of cutouts and stencils into slips and glazes, as in *Standing Jar,* 1954–56 (p. 121).[19] An exhibition of the paintings of Joan Miró in 1956 brought a brighter palette into play, encouraging Voulkos to experiment with low-fire glazes on stoneware. Later he began to add paint and epoxy to the surface, an act of heresy at the time and a break with the Arts and Crafts dictum of truth to materials.

The exhibition of Viennese sculptor Fritz Wotruba at the Los Angeles County Museum in 1955 sparked Voulkos's short-lived but notable exploration of ceramic sculpture. As Soldner remembers, after seeing Wotruba's show, "Pete went back to the studio and started stacking [thrown] rock-like forms. You could see the influence right away."[20] Voulkos had set up a separate studio, outside Otis, with John Mason, where the two made clay sculpture. Voulkos's stacks were a logical outgrowth from his pots, assembled from large thrown and altered forms, at first black (see *5000 Feet,* p. 12) and later painted in an abstract manner. Mason, meanwhile, truly took to this new genre. *Spear Form,* 1957 (p. 12), his first sculptural work, is a superbly articulated, mature piece that established his voice for the next decade.

In three years the Otis group had achieved two separate but related revolutions, liberating vessel forms from their decorative and utilitarian identity and creating a context for nonvessel ceramic sculpture. How did the L.A. art world react? One of the myths is that this group worked in isolation, disdained or ignored by the rest of the world. Price recalls of the early years, "We were getting it from all sides in those days. Fine arts people thought clay was stuck in limbo someplace and the crafts people hated this moving into a more expressive use of clay. They had a tough idea of function and they didn't like what we were doing. So we had a lot of freedom to operate—benign neglect."[21]

Benign neglect, however, lasted only a few years, and the record of exhibitions from 1956 onward offers a different picture. Otis work quickly found its way into the local fine-arts galleries, and during the sixties it was shown in major museums in both solo shows and significant group sculpture surveys. For art school students or recent graduates, the Otis group had a surprising number of opportunities and a great deal of support and encouragement, particularly in the lower, emerging echelons of the fine arts world. It is true that the East Coast and European museums, and certainly the trendsetting New York galleries, remained largely unaware of what was taking place in ceramics; and that few serious writers and critics were taking notice, aside from Rose Slivka, who started writing about the new clay in the craft press in the fifties, and John Coplans, who covered it in art journals in the early sixties.

In March 1957 the Ferus Gallery opened on La Cienega Boulevard in Los Angeles. The galley was founded as an artist's co-op by artist Ed Keinholz and curator Walter Hopps; later that year Irving Blum, one of the great dealers in postwar American art, joined them. By the sixties Blum had developed the gallery into a respected, cutting-edge venue. In the summer of 1957 Ferus showed work by Mason, Soldner, and Rothman and in later years gave regular solo shows to Mason (1957, 1959, 1961, and 1963) and Price (1960, 1961, and 1964). Andy Warhol had his first gallery exhibition at Ferus, which also introduced Jasper Johns, Roy Lichtenstein, Frank Stella, Joseph Cornell, and others to California. Ferus showcased major European artists such as Giorgio Morandi. Until it closed in 1966, this progressive space was the epicenter for the more radical local artists, including the masters of L.A. Style, Larry Bell, Craig Kauffman, Bill Irwin, and Ed Ruscha.

From 1956 Voulkos was represented in Los Angeles by the Felix Landau Gallery, which dealt mainly in sculpture by European modernist masters. He continued to win awards, including the Gold Medal at the International Ceramic Exposition in Cannes, France, 1955, and the Rodin Museum Prize in sculpture from the Museum of Modern Art, Paris, in 1959. In 1958 he was included in a survey of American contemporary art at the American Pavilion at the World's Fair in Brussels. He had nine one-person exhibitions between 1954 and 1960, culminating in a show at the members-only Penthouse Gallery of the Museum of Modern Art, New York, curated by Peter Selz.

Critical response was mixed. Letters to *Ceramics Monthly* in 1957 described Voulkos's pots as "chunks of stone, badly thrown, badly glazed and badly crafted."[22] But Slivka, Voulkos's champion and the editor of *Craft Horizons,* enthusiastically reviewed his solo show in 1957 at Bonniers (a small, progressive New York department store): "Voulkos has ventured courageously into a risky area for potters. That there is an ambivalence in his results is perhaps inevitable.... But Peter Voulkos the potter, Peter Voulkos the painter and Peter Voulkos the sculptor all make a fascinating pot and a controversial one."[23]

Locally the group was receiving a fair amount of attention, although serious collectors were definitely in short supply. For most of the Otis years the major patron was Fred Marer, a mathematics teacher of modest means who worked at a community college. He stumbled into the ceramics department one day in the spring of 1955 and was taken by what he saw. He consistently purchased work by the group (at the time the pieces sold for anything from a few dollars for a cup to a hundred dollars for a major work), and he provided encouragement, hosted dinners, and offered interest-free loans to see the artists through rough times.

Unfortunately, director Millard Sheets did not share the L.A. art community's growing enthusiasm for Otis clay. He had hoped Voulkos's graduates would make charming pots, and he had little sympathy for the radical direction they took instead. He objected to the influence of Picasso's ceramics, the large scale, the expletives scrawled on Billy Al Bengston's pots, and Voulkos's use of house paint on fired clay. When in 1956 Sheets accused the students of taking an "ivory tower" stance, Soldner, Frimkess, and a few others responded by opening a cooperative exhibition space, The Ivory Tower Gallery, in a leased storefront on Sunset Boulevard. Some of their exhibitions were reviewed in the *Los Angeles Times.* The gallery closed in 1957 but, as Mary Davis McNaughton writes, "it was an important expression of the independent thinking and self-reliance of the artists who worked with Voulkos."[24]

In December 1958, the roof of Otis's new building was set afire during a kiln firing. Sheets asked for Voulkos's resignation in May 1959. A month later Voulkos was hired as assistant professor of ceramics in the design department at the University of California, Berkeley. Later Sheets recalled the first two honeymoon years of Voulkos's reign at Otis as incredible: "He was at his height. His pots were magnificent.... [by 1957] the department was headed for the rocks. The respect for the medium, for the discipline, for what could be done in fine ceramics just went out of the window. And it was tragic."[25]

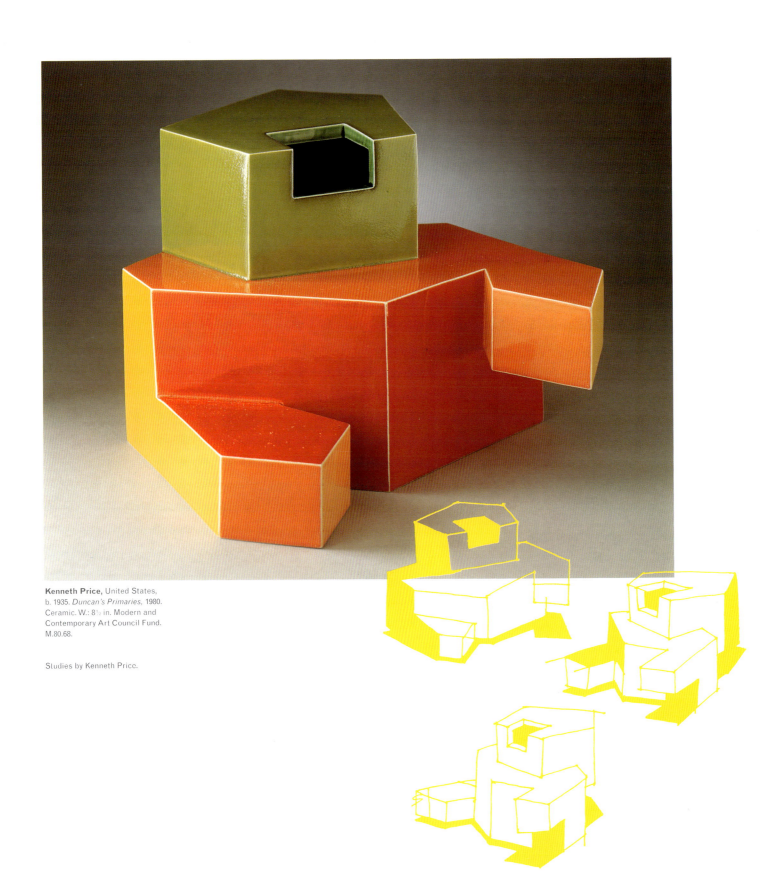

Kenneth Price, United States,
b. 1935. *Duncan's Primaries,* 1980.
Ceramic. W.: 8½ in. Modern and
Contemporary Art Council Fund.
M.80.68.

Studies by Kenneth Price.

Berkeley

Voulkos's move north to Berkeley marked the end of a period of innocence. At Otis, all limitations, rules, taboos and art-world politics had been blithely ignored or swept aside by a mixture of enthusiasm and naiveté. But by the time Voulkos arrived at Berkeley he was wiser. He was beginning to understand that the art world's resistance to ceramics as fine art ran deep and that trying to overcome it was likely to have a negative impact on his career. Also he found himself in a much larger school, albeit the most radical in the U.C. firmament, with a more competitive environment than the relatively unstructured and intimate world at Otis. His decisions and strategies were now, by necessity, more calculated.

His departure did not end the Otis clay laboratory. Voulkos kept a studio in Los Angeles until 1961. Shuttling between L.A. and Berkeley, his former students stayed in close touch, and in turn became friends and mentors to Voulkos's new students. But the Otis students also had to make real-world adjustments and navigate the art market to build their careers. The clay revolution in the early 1960s became more self-conscious and cautious, but it still had momentum. As the Otis artists moved in new directions, Voulkos's students at Berkeley made their own discoveries, and artists in other media were drawn into Voulkos's magnetic circle.

Of the Otis artists, Voulkos, Mason, and Henry Takemoto had made the greatest impact in the 1950s. Ken Price began to match their achievement after he earned a degree from Alfred University in 1959. Returning to Los Angeles, he set aside his Otis palette of blue-brown glazed stoneware and shifted to earthenware and low-fire glazes. New biomorphic elements reflected the influence of Hans Arp, Salvador Dalí, and other Surrealists. Conventional vases and plates gave way to organic lumps, egg forms, and cup forms (such as *Snail Cup,* 1968, this page). He worked in a sharp, acid-colored palette (using both glaze and automotive lacquer) that was distinctive, innovative, and vital. As Henry Hopkins wrote of Price's work in 1963, "Like the geometric redness of the Black Widow's belly or the burning rings of a Coral Snake, these objects proclaim their intent to survive."[26]

Kenneth Price, United States.
Snail Cup, 1968. Ceramic.
H.: 2⅞ in. Art Museum Council
Fund. M.83.230.60.

From the outset Price rejected any association with the crafts community. He insisted that his work be shown in art galleries, such as Ferus, where he was associated with other artists who developed the highly refined aesthetic and use of materials that became known as Finish Fetish or L.A. Style.

Mason also eschewed the crafts world. Attracted by the minimalism of Tony Smith and the young Conceptual movement, he concentrated on large-scale sculpture. His work became increasingly reductive, culminating in the dramatic, geometric, monochrome monoliths and metallic-glazed spear forms he showed at LACMA in 1966. He moved into a more conceptual realm in the 1970s with installations from the Hudson River series, six floor sculptures in fire brick for six museums. He then moved in the 1980s into a re-exploration of the vessel, first with his torque pots and then in the 1990s with vessels that explored a different sense of geometry in complex surface patterns and pentagonal shapes.

John Mason compacting clay on his easel for a large ceramic relief, in his studio on Glendale Boulevard, Los Angeles, 1959 or 1960. Photograph courtesy of John Mason.

Also in the 1960s Michael Frimkess began to create his "melting" pots, recognizable pottery shapes from various cultures (Greek volute kraters, Chinese ginger jars, American Indian Zuñi pots) covered in cartoonish images: cyclists rather than traditional runners on Greek vases, rampant Uncle Sams pursuing multihued women around ginger jars.

Soldner was more part of the crafts community and became one of the stars of the "workshop circuit," known for his lively demonstrations. He toured the country as something of a guru, popularizing his Americanized approach to the centuries-old Japanese raku technique. Rothman made beautiful sand-glazed vessels and was active through the 1980s with his so-called Bauhaus Baroque series of tureens, some phallic and powerfully organic and

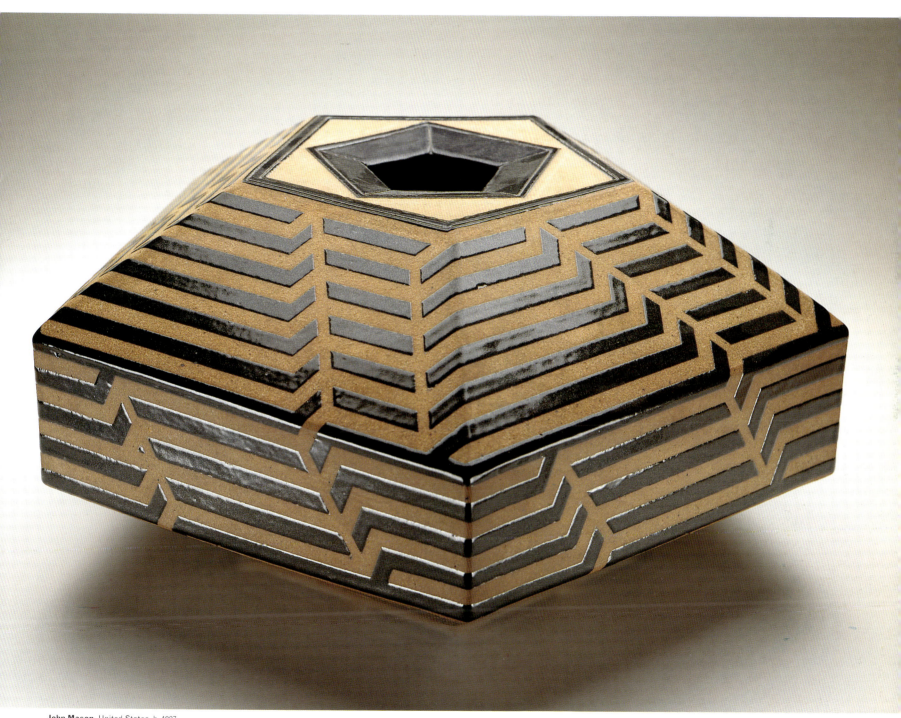

John Mason, United States, b. 1927.
Pentagonal Vessel, 1995. Stoneware.
H.: 9½ in. Smits Ceramics Purchase
Fund. AC1996.19.1.

others coolly geometric and Cubist, which are among the most significant signature forms of the decade. Billy Al Bengston left ceramics for a successful career as a painter. In 1957, Mac McClain moved to Mexico, taught in San Diego, then in 1995 moved back to L.A., where he taught for many years at Cal State L.A. In midcareer, McClain began to write poetry and criticism under the pen name of Mac McCloud. Sadly, Takemoto gave up ceramics early in the 1960s.

During the second phase of Voulkos's influence, from 1959 to 1966 at Berkeley, three more major artists emerged: Stephen De Staebler (b. 1933), James Melchert (b. 1930), and Ron Nagle (b. 1939) (again an all-male enclave). De Staebler can be seen as a spiritualist, Melchert a conceptualist, and Nagle a populist.

De Staebler's large-scale, totemic, fragmented figures, which resemble human fossils dug out of rock, are among the strongest in twentieth-century figural ceramics. Rather than portraits of individuals, they are everymen or everywomen, and their fragmentary structure gives them a vulnerability, as though, despite their solid form, born of rock and fire, they have been wounded and tested by life (see pp. 162–64). De Staebler studied theology at Princeton before joining Voulkos at Berkeley. Though he got along with Voulkos and his gang, he was not one of what Rose Slivka has called the "bad boys of ceramics." He is soft-spoken and enjoys quiet discussions about art and humanity. These qualities come across in his work. Prewar ceramic sculpture had been dominated by the precious tradition of the modestly scaled figurine. De Staebler's works were revolutionary in their large scale, their visual and emotional power, and their spirituality, and they had a profound influence on younger ceramists working with the human figure.

Melchert is responsible for an early 1960s masterpiece, *Leg Pot I,* 1962 (p. 146), made of slabbed and thrown clay, fabric, and lead. After graduating in 1961, he set out to free himself of the Abstract Expressionist influence he had inherited from Voulkos. In drawing classes he had become fixated with limbs and the way the arm or leg on a broken Greek torso would abruptly terminate in a cross section. Moreover, he had become impatient with "the conventions that seemed to tyrannize potters, the

Michael Frimkess applying a handle to a thrown, Greek-inspired vase form, with sketches behind him. Photograph © Leonard Nadel.

Jerry Rothman, United States,
b. 1933. *Skypot,* 1961. Stoneware.
H.: 20 in. Gift of Howard and
Gwen Laurie Smits. M.87.1.142.

vertical, bilaterally symmetrical structure of a vessel and the unquestioned acceptance of a single material."[27] His work became increasingly conceptual with each new series, from Ghostwares, 1967, to Games, 1971. After seeing Raymond Queneau's book *Exercises in Style,* shown in 1970 at the San Francisco Art Institute, Melchert began a series using the lower-case "a." The sculptures played a verbal-visual game with object and title: *Precious a* was small and glazed in gold, *Black a* was glazed black, *Pre-a* was made of unfired clay, and *a Made Forty Pounds Lighter* had handfuls of clay roughly gouged out of it. *Changes,* a 1972 performance piece in Amsterdam, which involved documenting the drying of slip on the human body, was the final step in his move toward the dematerialization of the ceramic object.

Counterclockwise, from left:
Jim Melchert with one of his A's in Berkeley, California, 1960. Photograph courtesy of Jim Melchert.

Jim Melchert, United States, b. 1930.

Leg Pot I, 1962. Stoneware, fired, with lead overlay. W.: approx. 30 in. Collection of the Museum of Contemporary Craft. Photograph courtesy of Jim Melchert.

Black A, 1982. Porcelain with glaze on lead-covered base. H.: 7 in. Purchased with funds provided by Friends of Clay and Decorative Arts Council. AC1999.29.2–.2

Nagle, enfant terrible of the Berkeley group, identified more closely with the Southern California movement than with the Bay Area art scene. He first saw slides of work done at Otis in 1958 at a workshop in San Francisco led by Henry Takemoto. Thereafter he made frequent trips to Los Angeles and his temple, the Ferus Gallery, missing few exhibitions in ten years. He was attracted to the sardonic quality, refined high-process approach, Pop Art edge, use of experimental and industrial materials, and vivid primary palette of L.A. Style. In 1961 he applied to join Berkeley's graduate ceramics program but was rejected. Voulkos, who identified with Nagle's youthful radicalism, circumvented the system by hiring him as a lab assistant.

Ron Nagle, United States, b. 1939. *Perfume Bottle,*
1960. Stoneware and low-fire glaze. H.: 24½ in.
Photograph © Don Tuttle, courtesy of Ron Nagle.

Ron Nagle in 1998. Photograph © Nigel Poor, courtesy of Ron Nagle.

Many in the Otis group influenced Nagle, but he found his kindred spirit in Price. He recalls first seeing Price's "little Grandma wares" at Ferus in 1960: "In this abstract expressionist realm, here is this guy making boxes with cups and lace and stuff and it blew my mind."[28] The large exhibition of Giorgio Morandi's drawings and paintings at Ferus in February 1961 also had a decisive impact. Here was an artist whose entire life's work was limited to painting and drawing a dozen intimate domestic objects on a few square feet of tabletop. This show gave Nagle the confidence to follow a narrow focus of his own. By 1963 he was making small, carefully articulated porcelain bottles and cups. He experimented with china paint, layering, and multiple firings to create rich, textured polychromatic surfaces. Within five years he had emerged as the most sophisticated colorist in American ceramics.

Peter Voulkos, United States, b. 1924. *Vase,* 1963. Stoneware with glazes. H.: 10½ in. Photograph courtesy of Peter Voulkos.

Peter Voulkos, United States, b. 1924. *Bottle/Vase,* 1961. Stoneware. H.: 18 in. Photograph courtesy of Peter Voulkos.

Voulkos, well acquainted with the local art world from his student days in Oakland, quickly became an inspirational, colorful fixture in the community. Nagle has commented that one learned more about art from watching Voulkos light a cigar than from watching him throw: "What I mean is that the guy has style.... It has nothing to do with fashion. It has to do with quality, the quality of being and with presence. He was such a heavy role model that everybody tried to emulate everything that he did, including his cigars and his brand of scotch and his pointed-toe flamenco boots."[29] Beyond his own students, Voulkos influenced Manuel Neri, Harold Paris, Wn Ng, and other emerging artists. According to Robert Arneson, Voulkos encouraged him to make the jump from "good" to "dirty" pottery and the feral, expressive energy of Funk.

Voulkos himself continued to do powerful work at Berkeley, modestly scaled, thick-walled vessels and torn and glaze-splashed plates. The pots he made between 1958 and 1963 represent a golden period in his oeuvre, as majestic and powerful as any in the modern history of the medium. But Voulkos got increasingly involved in working in metal at the school's foundry experiment. In 1963 he stopped working with ceramics altogether, and, except for a show of black vessels at Rena Bransten Gallery in San Francisco in 1968, did not return to the medium until the mid-1970s. Most recently he has been throwing and gas-firing plates and stack pots. While he has been playing with this composite form in various variations throughout his career, these works achieve a brooding mass and a dark presence unlike all the stacks that preceded them (see *Big Missoula,* p. 18).

John Coplans, who taught with Voulkos at Berkeley, contends that one of the reasons the artist turned to bronze was anguish that his ceramic work was not taken seriously.[30] Whatever the motivation, the fledgling avant-garde movement in ceramics had, for the moment, lost its leader.

Opposite:
Ron Nagle, United States, b. 1939. *My Compliments,* 1988. Earthenware, glazed. H.: 22 in. Gift of Rena Bransten and Charles Cowles in honor of Betty Asher. M.89.34.

Peter Voulkos, United States, b. 1924.
Large Plate, 1979. Stoneware. Diam.:
21½ in. Gift of Howard and Gwen
Laurie Smits. M.87.1.176.

Early Critical Reception and a Reassessment

California's breakthrough ceramics in the 1950s had been mainly regional. Most exhibitions took place either in Los Angeles or San Francisco, with reviews in local papers and some minor press nationally in the craft publications. But by the 1960s the group had found its two eloquent and loyal champions, Rose Slivka at *Craft Horizons* and John Coplans, a painter, educator, and editor at large for *Artforum.*

Slivka was a forceful writer and an intimate of the artists in the New York School. She challenged ceramics orthodoxy in issue 4, 1961, of *Craft Horizons,* with a manifesto entitled "The New Ceramic Presence," introducing her readers to the work of Voulkos and his students and connecting their style to what the New York action painters were doing. She made a compelling argument for change: "We are now groping for a new aesthetic to meet the needs of our time, or perhaps it is a new anti-aesthetic to break visual patterns that no longer suffice."[31]

Many of Slivka's readers, primarily members of the American Craft Council, which published the magazine, were shocked, seeing Voulkos and company as vandals out to destroy the refinement and elegance of the potter's art. They disliked what they saw as sloppy craft and a seemingly arbitrary aesthetic predicated on risk and intuition. Most preferred the safety, formality, and orderliness of prewar European decorative pottery or traditionally based Anglo-Asian ceramics à la Leach. The article caused a furor, and some members of the council even resigned in protest. Ironically, the field has since evolved to the point where it is sometimes difficult today to convince younger ceramists that the work of Voulkos and his students was *ever* a radical statement.

Coplans also admired Voulkos's work and considered him "more interesting than anyone in the [Berkeley] Art department" where they both taught.[32] In 1963, with Paul Mills, director of the Oakland Museum, and Walter Hopps, then a curator at the Pasadena Art Museum, Coplans curated a survey at the Kaiser Centre, *Sculpture of California.* Among the fifty sculptures selected, eleven were ceramics by De Staebler, Frimkess, Mason, Melchert, Ng, Price, and Voulkos.

View of the exhibition *Abstract Expressionist Ceramics,* curated by John Coplans, at the University of California, Irvine, in 1966.

"Sculpture in California," Coplans's lead article in the August 1963 issue of the one-year-old *Artforum*, focused on the ceramic works. A livid red Price sculpture graced the front cover and an installation photograph on the back featured Voulkos's *Little Big Horn.* For the next three years Coplans wrote frequently in *Artforum, Art in America,* and *Art International* about this new ceramics movement and continued to include the artists in the exhibitions he organized. He also wrote the catalogue for John Mason's 1966 exhibition of his sculpture at LACMA.

But the breakthrough moment arrived with Coplans's exhibition *Abstract Expressionist Ceramics,* organized for the Art Gallery, University of California, Irvine (October 28 to November 27, 1966), and the Museum of Modern Art, San Francisco (January 11 to February 12, 1967). The exhibition included the work of Mason, Voulkos, Melchert, McClain, Nagle, and Price, as well as sculptor Manuel Neri. It stunned and excited the ceramics world and caused those who had previously dismissed ceramics as a therapeutic activity, like finger painting, to rethink its potential. American ceramists, no longer shackled by the Asian and European traditions, now had a lively movement of their own and a plastic, muscular new language. The excellent catalogue essay by Coplans became one of the most important texts in the field.

Three decades later, the legacy of this groundbreaking exhibition can be more clearly assessed. It is clear that Coplans chose his art and artists well. Many of the featured objects, including Melchert's *Leg Pot I,* 1962 (p. 146), and *Plate with Muffin Tin,* 1963, Voulkos's *Bottle/Vase,* 1961 (p. 148), which was illustrated as the frontispiece of the catalogue, and Mason's *X-Pot,* 1957 (p. 155), and several others, have since been canonized as masterworks. All of the featured artists have continued as prominent players in both the crafts and the fine arts.

The title of the exhibition had a great deal to do with its powerful effect. It took the work out of the crafts closet and decisively placed it in a fine-arts context, where these artists' radical handling of clay and glaze could be understood in terms of the painting of De Kooning, Kline, and Pollock. Unfortunately, however, the name *Abstract Expressionist Ceramics* also did the work and the artists a disservice and has led to lasting misunderstanding. By positioning California ceramics as "the most ingenious regional adaptation of the spirit of Abstract Expressionism that has yet emerged,"[33] Coplans relegated it to a Johnny-come-lately passenger on the Abstract Expressionist bandwagon then rolling through American art.

Abstract Expressionism influenced only some of the Otis and Berkeley artists, and not until well after the movement had begun. As Coplans correctly states, "the peak of the ceramic development was undoubtedly between the years 1956 and 1958."[34] In those years the Otis aesthetic was defined. But it was not until 1958 that Voulkos developed his interest in the work of the action painters. That year he was invited to New York by Slivka and again met with De Kooning, Kline, and others. Up until this point his and his students' muses had been Europeans: Picasso, Miró, Wotruba, the Surrealists, Morandi, and Joseph Cornell. Fred Marer, a consistent witness at the Otis studios, states that there was no strong Abstract Expressionist influence discernible before 1958.[35] Voulkos did not mention the New York School of painters in any of his article or interviews until after 1958. Mason has said that his own first and last consciously Abstract Expressionist works were wall pieces he made in 1958 by trailing long, thin slabs of clay over each other.

Some of the works in *Abstract Expressionist Ceramics,* particularly Voulkos's later works, fit comfortably (Abstract Expressionism became a primary influence for Voulkos in the early 1960s, although he continued to draw from other sources, such as Lucio Fontana's ceramics

Opposite:
Paul Soldner, United States, b. 1921. *Wasp-Waist Form,* 1982. Earthenware, thrown and altered, salt fired. H.: 15½ in. Gift of Howard and Gwen Laurie Smits. M.87.1.158.

from the Concetto Spaziale series). Most, however, did not belong. In conversation in the spring of 1976, Coplans agreed that the Abstract Expressionist umbrella was perhaps not watertight, although "it seemed convenient at the time."[36] Slivka also conceded in conversation in 1997 that she had overstated the influence of action painting on the Otis group.

But the myth has been perpetuated ever since. In 1981 Suzanne Foley wrote that the movement's "beginnings in the mid-1950s were a *direct* response to Abstract Expressionist painting."[37] In his book *Sunshine Muse,* Peter Plagens writes, "Voulkos and his students managed the redoubtable feat of removing the craft of ceramics to the province of sculpture by overcoming a dependence on the potter's wheel, by slab-building, denting, cracking, and only partially glazing—in short, by creating a Southern California Abstract Expressionist ceramics."[38] As I have argued above, the potter's wheel played a central role at Otis, and the slab-building, denting, cracking, and partial glazing were borrowed from traditional Japanese ceramics.

The now-canonical name Abstract Expressionist ceramics distorts what these artists achieved: an original, indigenous new art movement rooted in many influences: mud, fire, utility, social and art history, Zen, jazz, Haniwa figures, tea ceremony wares, Greek classical vases, Picasso's ceramics, pottery from the Scandinavian Moderne movement, contemporary sculpture, pop culture, and yes, Abstract Expressionist as well as other styles of painting.

John Mason, United States, b. 1927. *X-Pot,* 1957. H.: 14 in. Photograph © Frank J. Thomas, courtesy of John Mason.

Opposite:
Paul Soldner, United States, b. 1921. *84–45 Pedestal Piece,* 1984. Clay, salt fired. H.: 17 in. Gift of Joel and Judith Slutzky. M.84.109.

In 1982 Christopher Knight, in a review of the exhibition *Otis Clay: The Revolutionary Years 1954–64* (Garth Clark Gallery, Los Angeles, September 1982), wrote that the ceramics of the time had been wrapped in "unfounded and uncritically held beliefs" and that the time had arrived for honest reappraisal: "While it can not be denied that a good deal of this ceramic work was created with a concern for sculptural values and with an awareness of contemporaneous developments in Abstract Expressionist painting, the 'revolution' which occurred in Otis in the late 1950s is not to be found in ceramics attempting to mimic the conventions—long held or newly held—of either sculpture or painting. Rather it was a revolution within the tradition of pottery itself."[39]

As Coplans concluded in *Abstract Expressionist Ceramics,* these artists were able to "totally revolutionize the approach to ceramics.... What was done in those days is now mainstream ceramics."[40] The time has come to reevaluate this achievement on its own terms, identifying its masterworks and thoroughly examining its evolution and aesthetic principles. A deeper understanding of this movement, with its originality, independent-minded artists, tough and majestic art, flashes of pure genius, and mold-breaking radicalism, would seem well worth the effort.

Garth Clark is the author of eighteen books and numerous monographs on ceramics. He received the Art Critics Award from the National Endowment for the Arts and the Art Book of the Year award from the Art Libraries Society of North America for *The Mad Potter of Biloxi: The Art and Life of George E. Ohr.* He was made a Fellow of the Royal College of Art for his contribution to scholarship in ceramics and in 1999 received the Visionaries: Lifetime Achievement Award from the American Craft Museum.

Notes

1 For more on the Super-Object see my book *American Ceramics: 1876 to the Present* (New York: Abbeville, 1990), 153–54.

2 I am indebted to Ken Ferguson, who replaced Voulkos at the Archie Bray Foundation, for drawing my attention to this body of work. A few years ago I passed one of these bowls around a group of visiting Japanese potters and asked them their opinion. They admired the vigor in the throwing but pointed out that the bowl was too high. The bamboo whisk for the powdered tea used in the tea ceremony is a standard height, and all Japanese tea bowls are scaled accordingly. Having no experience of the tea ceremony, Voulkos made up his own rules, a freedom from and indifference to conventions that he and his students exercised frequently.

3 For a tough, revisionist view of Leach's philosophy and his understanding of Japanese and Asian art, see Edmund De Waal, *Bernard Leach* (London: Tate Gallery Publishing, 1998).

4 Oliver Watson, *Studio Pottery: Twentieth Century British Ceramics in the Victoria and Albert Museum Collection* (London: Phaidon Press in association with Victoria and Albert Museum, 1993), 15.

5 Bernard Leach, *A Potter's Outlook* (London: Handworkers Pamphlet No. 3, 1928). Reprinted in Carol Hogben, ed., *The Art of Bernard Leach* (New York: Watson Guptill, 1978).

6 Bernard Leach, "American Impressions," *Craft Horizons* 10, no. 4 (winter 1950): 18–20.

7 Suzanne Foley, "Ceramic Sculpture in California: An Overview," in Richard Marshall and Suzanne Foley, *Ceramic Sculpture: Six Artists,* exh. cat. (New York: Whitney Museum of American Art, 1981), 10.

8 Mac McCloud [McClain had adopted the pen name of McCloud by this time], "Otis Clay: 1956–1957," *Ceramic Arts,* no. 1 (spring 1983): 2.

9 Peter Voulkos quoted in Conrad Brown, "Peter Voulkos," *Craft Horizons* 16, no. 5 (September/October 1956): 12.

10 Ibid.

11 Mary Davis MacNaughton, "Innovation in Clay: The Otis Era 1954–1960," in *Revolution in Clay: The Marer Collection of Contemporary Ceramics* (Claremont, Calif.: Ruth Chandler Williamson Gallery, Scripps College; Seattle and London: University of Washington Press, 1994), 61.

12 Paul Soldner quoted in "West Coast Ceramics," *Craft Horizons* 26, no. 3 (June 1966): 27. This article is a dialogue between Soldner and Voulkos recalling the early years at Otis and Berkeley. Asked if he remembered the name of the pot Voulkos replied, "Yeah, 'Love Is a Many Splendored Thing.' I showed it in my show at the Felix Landau Gallery in Los Angeles in 1956, and it was sold.... pottery at this point began to be noticed by painters and sculptors."

13 See, for example, Edy de Wilde's preface to Rose Slivka, *West Coast Ceramics* (Amsterdam: Stedelijk Museum, 1979), 1. De Wilde denies the roots and traditions of the potter in Voulkos's work. He writes that Voulkos's vessels only "look like pots," but that one must not be deceived, "for their sole purpose seemed to be the visualization of volume and form— sculpture in other words." In his haste to separate Voulkos from the craft of pottery, de Wilde ignores the "visualization of volume and form" that has been the core aesthetic of the potter for more than 10,000 years.

14 Picasso quoted in Daniel-Henry Kahnweiler, *Picasso's Ceramics* (Hanover: Fackelträger, 1957), 17.

15 Peter Voulkos quoted in Rose Slivka, *Peter Voulkos* (Boston: New York Graphic Society, 1978), 12.

16 Elaine Levin, interview with Vivika and Otto Heino, Archives of American Art, 4 March 1981.

17 See MacNaughton, 60.

18 Ken Price quoted in MacNaughton, 55.

19 MacNaughton, 60.

20 Paul Soldner quoted in MacNaughton, 61.

21 Ken Price quoted in Susan Wechsler, *Low-Fire Ceramics: A New Direction in American Clay* (New York: Watson-Guptill, 1981), 113.

22 Letters to *Ceramics Monthly* quoted by Neil Benezra in *Robert Arneson: A Retrospective,* exh. cat. (Des Moines: Des Moines Art Center, 1986), 14.

23 Rose Slivka, "Peter Voulkos at Bonniers," *Craft Horizons* 17, no. 2 (March/April 1957): 47.

24 MacNaughton, 57.

25 Millard Sheets, "Los Angeles Art Community: Group Portrait," interview by George M. Goodwin, Oral History Program, UCLA, 1997, 330–31; quoted in MacNaughton, 70, n. 54.

26 Henry Hopkins, "Kenneth Price: Untitled Ceramic," *Artforum* 2 (August 1963): 41.

27 Jim Melchert quoted in Lee Nordness, *Objects: USA* (New York: Viking, 1970), 121.

28 Ron Nagle quoted in Barbaralee Diamonstein, *Handmade in America* (New York: Abrams, 1983), 169.

29 Ibid, 178.

30 John Coplans, letter to author, 12 May 1997.

31 Rose Slivka, "The New Ceramic Presence," *Craft Horizons* 21, no. 4 (July/August 1961); reprinted in Garth Clark, ed. *Ceramic Art: Comment and Review, 1882–1977* (New York: E. P. Dutton, 1978), 142.

32 Coplans, letter to author, 12 May 1997.

33 Coplans, "Abstract Expressionist Ceramics," in *Abstract Expressionist Ceramics,* exh. cat. (Irvine, Calif.: Art Gallery, University of California, Irvine, 1966), 7.

34 Ibid., 16.

35 Fred Marer, letter to author, January 1977.

36 John Coplans, interview with author, January 1977.

37 Foley, 10.

38 Peter Plagens, *Sunshine Muse* (New York: Praeger, 1974), 95.

39 Christopher Knight, "Otis Clay: A Revolution in the Tradition of Pottery," *Los Angeles Herald Examiner,* 29 September 1982, E5.

40 Coplans, *Abstract Expressionist Ceramics,* 16.

Richard Shaw, United States, b. 1941. *Happy Birthday,* 1996. Porcelain, glazed, with overglaze decals. H.: 69½ in. Smits Ceramics Purchase Fund. AC1998.10.1.1–.24.

Study by Richard Shaw.

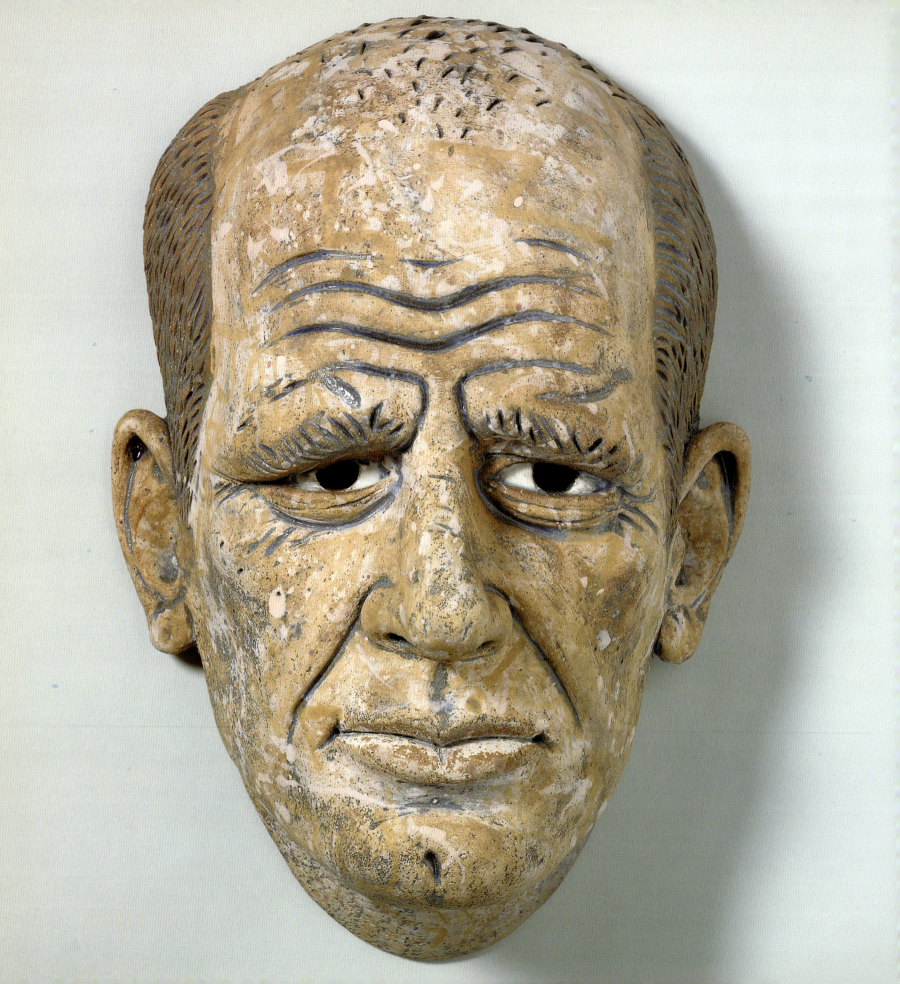

The Figurative Impulse in Contemporary Ceramics

PETER SELZ

Peter Voulkos working on a large ceramic sculpture, 1960. Photograph courtesy of Peter Voulkos.

Opposite:
Robert Arneson, United States, 1930–1992. *Jackson Pollock,* 1983. Earthenware. H.: 15 in. Gift of Howard and Gwen Laurie Smits. M.87.1.9.

Ancient civilizations produced figurative works in clay that tell us about their everyday lives, fears, hopes, and deities. Only in very recent history, during the dominance of the bourgeoisie, has clay been excluded from high art, perhaps because of its humble origins. Its revival as a sculptural medium in the mid-twentieth century was to a great extent due to the innovative ceramics made by Peter Voulkos (b. 1924) in Los Angeles in the 1950s. Before that time, the concept that work in clay must be utilitarian was not questioned, and ceramics was a field marked by distinguished craftsmanship rather than innovation. Ever since, artists have been exploiting the flexible possibilities of clay to create figurative sculpture.

Viola Frey, United States, b. 1933. *Sky Blue Suit,* 1982. Ceramic on steel base. H.: 98½ in. Smits Ceramics Purchase Fund. AC1997.117.1.1-.6.

Michael Frimkess, United
States, b. 1937. *CFS004 Plate,*
1962. Earthenware. Diam.: 21 in.
Smits Ceramics Purchase
Fund. M.90.98.

When I first saw Voulkos's gigantic ceramic pieces at his studio on
Glendale Boulevard in Los Angeles in 1957, I was stunned. I had never
seen clay made into such powerful work as these stoneware pieces with
their strong color glazes. They were overwhelming in their sheer physical
presence and enigmatic in their technical fabrication. In 1959, as curator
of painting and sculpture at the Museum of Modern Art, New York, I was
appointed U.S. Commissioner of the *Première Biennale de Paris* and
included three large works by Voulkos, who received the Rodin Museum
prize for his *Sitting Bull,* c. 1959. A year later I curated a small solo show
of six sculptures and six canvases by Voulkos in MoMA's Penthouse
Gallery. Here was the work of the man who, by enlarging his vessels and,
most importantly, denying any utilitarian function, had changed the craft
of pottery into the art of clay sculpture.

Voulkos had been inspired by Franz Kline and the Abstract
Expressionist painters, and by Philip Guston, Robert Rauschenburg,
and others. Affected also by his study of Zen, he valued process and
accident in his work. Although his vertical stoneware stacks have no
overt anthropomorphic elements, they are clearly informed by figurative

sculpture from Asia and Europe, from the past and present. He was particularly influenced by Japanese Haniwa sculpture, primitive but expressive earthenware figures placed on royal burial tombs from about 300 to 600 A.D.[1] Among modernist works Voulkos admired Picasso's painted bronze and ceramic figures and the inventive, multivalent ceramic sculpture that Miró produced with the fine ceramics craftsman Llorens Artigas. He also expressed great interest in the sculpture of Fritz Wotruba, which he saw in 1955. (For an illustration of a sculpture by Wotruba, see p. 16.) He has spoken about the Austrian sculptor's method of stacking his bronzes,[2] but he must also have been aware of the universal quality of Wotruba's androgynous figures.

At the Los Angeles County Art Institute (later renamed the Otis Art Institute) during the 1950s, Voulkos taught a group of students who quickly emerged as important artists, including Paul Soldner, John Mason, Kenneth Price, and Michael Frimkess. (For more about the work of these Otis artists, see the essay by Garth Clark herein, p. 123.) The youngest of the group, Frimkess (b. 1937), has used figuration in his surface decoration. For example, *CFS004 Plate,* 1982 (opposite), is incised with primitive human profiles, evocative of children's drawings, and mysterious numbers, and has the rough-looking, asymmetric shape that Frimkess and his Otis colleagues admired in Japanese raku pottery.

In 1959 Voulkos was appointed to the faculty of the Art Department at the University of California, Berkeley. His audacious work there further subverted the prevailing purist taboos that had restricted clay to the making of useful pottery and opened the way for new discoveries by artists such as Harold Paris (1925–1979). When Paris arrived in Berkeley to join the art faculty in 1960, the largely self-taught artist was already well known as a printmaker and had recently begun to make bronze sculpture. During the war he had been assigned by the newspaper *Stars and Stripes* to go to the death camp at Buchenwald. This experience found its reverberations in his *Hosanna Suite,* a graphic cycle of etchings, aquatints, and lithographs, poignant visions of life, tragedy, and death.

Harold Paris, United States, 1925–1979. *Wall III,* 1962. Fired ceramic, 90 x 156 x 48 in. Photograph courtesy of Deborah Little Paris.

Stephen De Staebler in his studio,
working on the figurative sculpture
Seated Woman with Mimbres Womb,
c. 1978. Photograph by Karl H. Riek.

At Berkeley Paris saw Voulkos working in the "Pot Palace," a makeshift basement studio, and was inspired to explore the possibilities of clay. He began creating monumental walls, made of many separate pieces, in which he translated much of the imagery of the *Hosanna Suite*—with its dramatic anxiety and intimate sexuality—into powerful and energetic reliefs. He named these impressive structures *Walls for Mem,* after *mem,* the thirteenth letter of the Hebrew alphabet; three "m" places where he had lived (Majorca, Madrid, and Munich); and Malach, Hebrew for the Angel of Death. He completed the first Wall in a twenty-four-hour period of nonstop activity, dramatically grabbing, twisting, cutting, and gouging the clay. *Wall III* 1962 (p. 161), the last of the group, done with more deliberation, is a great technical accomplishment, almost nine feet tall. (In Los Angeles John Mason had made an even larger ceramic wall in 1960, but without human imagery.) With their bulging humanoid elements, Paris's Walls seem to invade the viewer's space. Executed with exuberant passion, they convey what Jackson Pollock may have meant when he spoke of energy made visible in art. The critic Jerome Tarshis concluded, "More allusive than realistic, [Paris's] walls offer hints of ruined structures and fragmented bodies. Paris managed to bring the Surrealists' interest in psychology and their imaginative treatment of the human body, the concern of postwar European artists to reflect the horrors of war, and the Abstract Expressionists' freedom of design."[3]

Stephen De Staebler (b. 1933) arrived at Voulkos's program in Berkeley in 1959 after studying theology at Princeton. He was influenced by Voulkos and also by Paris's ceramic walls, with their incipient figuration,

Stephen De Staebler, United States, b. 1933. *Seated Woman with Mimbres Womb,* 1978. Clay, fired. H.: 71 in. Smits Ceramics Purchase Fund and Gift of Dr. Jay Cooper. AC1997.88.1.1–.3.

which he said "made a strong impression on me, particularly in their tendency to digress to random forms…[The Walls] were powerful works, and to my eye, the most fully realized imagery. Realized, not in the sense of refinement, but in their fully tactile presence."[4] Soon, according to Thomas Albright, De Staebler "became the most original and powerful clay sculptor of the [Berkeley] group."[5] In 1967 he was commissioned by the Newman Center in Berkeley to design and build a sanctuary, an architectural and sculptural work of liturgical elements. The result, a manifest triumph of clay sculpture in our time, encourages meditation with its judicious placement of objects and austere simplicity. The crucifix is made of high-fired clay and set high on a wall. The sanctuary itself is designed to resemble landscapes in its depressions and rises, contrasting with the crucifix's vertical aspiration.

Both this work and De Staebler's later figurative pieces exploit the essential character of clay: its unpredictable performance in the artist's hands, its wetness when soft and leathery toughness when hardened, its tendency to crack—in short, its truly organic, earthbound quality. His fragmentary figures with their encrusted surfaces recall the static presence of ancient Egyptian sculpture or resemble the eroded survivors of unknown prehistoric civilizations. *Seated Woman with Mimbres Womb,* 1978 (p. 163), suggests the artist's desire to connect a contemporary sensibility to human history. The stacked segments are joined by gravity in the archaic form of the stele; the rounded opening refers to the cavities in the pottery of the Native American Mimbres group.

During the 1980s De Staebler created fragmentary, androgynous winged figures in bronze as well as clay. Incomplete, they convey the precarious quality of life, especially the existential alienation felt by men and women in our time. In a series of human legs made in the 1990s, De Staebler achieved subtle colors by blending pigment with the clay as well as by applying paint to the finished surface. He reduced these fragments to a modest scale in *Three Legs with Sliced Foot,* 1996 (opposite), disembodied, broken legs that nonetheless convey a poignant sense of human endurance. De Staebler's use of the primal matter of earthenware affirms life's processes of emergence and metamorphosis.

Stephen De Staebler, United States, b. 1933. *Crucifix, Sanctuary of the Holy Spirit Chapel, The Newman Center, Berkeley, California,* 1967–68. Stoneware. Photograph by Karl H. Riek.

In the San Francisco Bay Area during the early 1960s a new group of ceramists emerged, artists who took it for granted that clay could be used for nonutilitarian purposes. They looked at popular culture for many of their motifs, but in a manner very different from the New York Pop artists, who often created easily recognizable works that would have a ready appeal in the expanding New York art market. The chief artist of this group was the authentic iconoclast Robert Arneson (1930–1992). Arneson first studied at the California College of Arts and Crafts (CCAC) in Oakland, where he was still engaged in producing serviceable pots. Then, as a graduate student at Mills College (1957–58), also in Oakland, he encountered the work of Voulkos, and his work took a more radical direction. While demonstrating throwing pots at the California State Fair in Sacramento in 1961, he sealed a bottle with a clay cap and wrote the slogan *No Deposit* on its body. He called the piece *No Return* (p. 166). With this symbolic act, he suggested that clay's recent history as a medium merely for mass-produced commercial wares was over. In 1962 he arrived at the University of California, Davis, and before long was the head of the ceramics section there.

The art historian and ceramist Seymour Howard had created a small studio at Davis, which Arneson converted into the now-legendary TB-9 (Temporary Building 9) workshop. As Arneson's former student Richard Notkin recalled, "TB-9 was a microcosm of these times [the Hippie era]. Anarchy reigned. No overwhelming structure or 'curriculum' to hamper or impede your creative flow. We just worked, and we worked damn hard. We were a ragtag bunch—a loose group of mud-smeared hairy humans who hung around together—sharing an affinity for making clay into something we hoped would be Art. In short, TB-Niners."[6] According to Notkin, he and the other students at TB-9—among them artists as different as Richard Shaw and Peter VandenBerge, as well as Bruce Nauman, Deborah Butterfield, John Buck, and Steven Kaltenbach—learned from Arneson primarily through osmosis.

Stephen De Staebler, United States, b. 1933. *Three Legs with Sliced Foot,* 1996. Clay, fired. H.: 24 in. Gift of Mr. and Mrs. Paul LeBaron Thiebaud. AC1999.110.1.

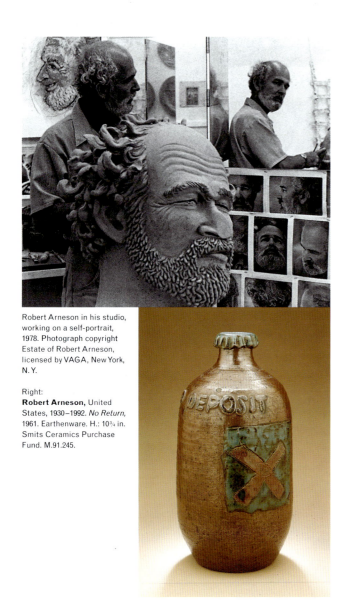

Robert Arneson in his studio, working on a self-portrait, 1978. Photograph copyright Estate of Robert Arneson, licensed by VAGA, New York, N.Y.

Right:
Robert Arneson, United States, 1930–1992. *No Return,* 1961. Earthenware. H.: 10¾ in. Smits Ceramics Purchase Fund. M.91.245.

Work created at Davis, as well as related sculpture and painting done elsewhere in the Bay Area, made without much regard for material or form, was bizarre, often quite ugly and ungainly, yet sensuous. This particular impudent, playful sensibility—which became known as Funk—was unique to the Bay Area. It had its roots in the Beat culture of the previous decade but was also a result of the isolation the artists in this region felt. As Harold Paris explained in an article for *Art in America,* "The serious artists, galleries and museums founder in this 'Bay' of lethargy and social inertia. The artist here is aware that no one really sees his work, and no one really supports it. So, in effect, he says 'Funk.' But also he is free. There is less pressure to 'make it.' The casual, irreverent, insincere California atmosphere, with its absurd elements— weather, clothes, 'skinny-dipping,' hobby craft, sun-drenched mentality, Doggie Diner, perfumed toilet tissue, do-it-yourself—all this drives the artist's vision inward. This is the land of Funk."[7]

Aware of this new attitude (it certainly was not a school or movement), I organized an exhibition and published a catalogue called *Funk* at the University Art Museum in Berkeley in 1967.[8] The exhibition included representatives from Davis (Arneson, William T. Wiley, Roy de Forest, and David Gilhooly); Berkeley (Paris, Voulkos, and James Melchert); and San Francisco (Bruce Conner, Robert Hudson, Joan Brown, Manuel Neri, and Peter Saul). Years later Funk was canonized in *The History of American Ceramics,* where Elaine Levin wrote, "Unlike Dadaism, which aspired to change the world, Funk's intentions were to change the perception of the world by putting familiar objects in an unfamiliar context so that they could be seen afresh."[9]

Arneson was the exemplary Funk artist, at least as far as his early work is concerned. In 1963 he made a series of clay toilets with turdlike handles and unflushed bowls, johns a great deal more shocking than the ironic soft-vinyl toilets that Claes Oldenburg made two years later. Arneson's *Typewriter,* 1965, with its keys of highly polished red fingernails, signifying the woman as a writing machine, is widely reproduced and has become a sort of standard for Funk. Once clay had been freed from the concepts of honesty and truth (propounded by potters such as Bernard Leach, Shōji Hamada, and Marguerite Wildenhain), the range of its uses became greatly amplified. Arneson continued to explore this new freedom, influenced by a broad range of artists in different media, including Franz Xaver Messerschmidt, Edvard Munch, and Pablo Picasso. In the 1970s he turned to portraiture and self-portraiture. In the large technical feat *Smorgi-Bob the Cook,* 1971, he depicts himself as a chef with a vast display of edibles, all in carefully manipulated perspective. In *Classical Exposure,* 1972, he appears on top of a classical urn with his genitals exposed. In 1982, in response to a disparaging review of an exhibition of California ceramics at the Whitney Museum,[10] Arneson created *California Artist,* a self-portrait in slovenly clothing, standing on a pedestal with a marijuana plant. Later he portrayed himself on the capital of an Ionic column with a pronounced twinkle in his eye and called the piece *Way West of Athens,* 1983 (right).

Robert Arneson, United States, 1930–1992. *Way West of Athens,* 1983. Bronze on ceramic base. H.: 73 in. The Harry and Yvonne Lenart Fund. M.85.63a–b.

Richard Notkin, United States, b. 1948. *Vain Imaginings,* c. 1978–79. Earthenware, glaze, and brass (T.V. antenna), on redwood and white cedar base. H.: 16 in. Gift of Howard and Gwen Laurie Smits. M.87.1.117a–e.

Known for his work as a portraitist, Arneson was commissioned in 1981 by the San Francisco Art Commission to make a bust of the assassinated mayor George Moscone for the city's new convention center. This splendid bust caused a great deal of public controversy. Below the grinning ceramic likeness, on the pedestal, Arneson inscribed references to the mayor's life and the so-called Twinkie defense used by Moscone's assassin, Dan White. The bust was removed in an unforgivable act of censorship, but it brought Arneson international recognition. Shortly thereafter, feeling an increasing sense of identification with Jackson Pollock, Arneson made a series of sculptures, paintings, and drawings of the iconic American painter (see p. 158). Toward the end of his life he confronted the danger of nuclear war in his work. According to the critic Donald Kuspit, "his nuclear imagery sharply focuses the fact that there is one serious issue in art today: the re-connection of art and morality—the reconceiving of art as a form of moral politics."[11]

Moral politics is also a defining issue in the work of Arneson's former student Richard Notkin (b. 1948). From a very early age Notkin was inspired by films on Nazi concentration camps to create work with political meaning. Playful, with an intricacy inspired by Chinese Yixing teapots, his works resemble political cartoons in their use of metaphor and allegory. In his Endangered Species series, begun in 1978, Notkin expressed antiwar and other political and social messages, frequently using human skulls of precisely crafted porcelain. In *Vain Imaginings,* c. 1978–79 (opposite), for example, he placed a ceramic skull on books atop a fastidiously made chess set. The skull looks at its reflection on a television screen, topped by a book, titled *The Shallow Life,* which in turn serves as the base of a coke bottle and a cactus plant. The composition is an evocative version of the traditional memento mori.

Notkin is one of a number of important artists, including Richard Shaw, Marilyn Levine, and Elaine Carhartt, who take advantage of the unlimited pliancy of clay to produce illusionist or trompe l'oeil sculptures. Richard Shaw (b. 1941), the son of a Walt Disney animator, was trained as a painter and then studied sculpture at the San Francisco Art Institute before he arrived at Davis in 1967. He remembers TB-9 as a "place of radiating energy."[12] His work often seems to reflect the cartoon illusionism of Disney movies. To achieve fine detail, he turned to porcelain, which is capable of highly realistic renderings and, fired at high temperatures, yields painterly surfaces. Shaw replicated everyday objects to create startling trompe-l'oeil still lifes. He has also made whimsical, anthropomorphic little statues, such as *Happy Birthday,* 1996 (p. 157). This highly imaginative, striding stick figure—a rather scary birthday guest—has a leg that resembles a tree trunk and a skull wearing a foolscap and offers an apple pierced with sharp pencils, every element precisely rendered in deceptive clay.

Born in Canada in 1935, Marilyn Levine did her graduate work at Berkeley with Voulkos and his group. She specializes in replicating leather goods in stoneware. Her shoes, jackets, suitcases and bags, with all of their scuffs and other marks of human use, are so realistic that the viewer questions his or her perception. Elaine Carhartt (b. 1951) grew up in Colorado and studied in Mexico before settling in Pasadena, where she now produces playful, whimsical creatures of droll humor, such as *Queen*, 1980 (opposite), a smiling lady riding a fantasy cart, made of bisque clay and then painted brightly with acrylic. This genre in ceramics is comparable to the work of contemporaneous East Coast sculptors Duane Hanson and John de Andrea and related to the work of Super- or Photorealist painters such as Richard Estes, Robert Bechtle, and Ralph Goings. It also comprehends and reaffirms the tradition of the American trompe-l'oeil still-life painters William Harnett and John Peto. Its attitude is very much in keeping with contemporary theory: The French poststructuralist sociologist Jean Baudrillard postulates that in the current era the very excess of images leads the artist to the creation of simulacra and implies that there is no substantial difference between reality and fiction.

Other former students of Arneson, such as Peter VandenBerge and Robert Brady, shared their teacher's preoccupation with the human figure, which they often disfigure or refigure in their sculpture. VandenBerge, born in Holland in 1935, moved with his parents to the Dutch East Indies, then escaped to Australia during World War II before settling in California. Working with Funk artist David Gilhooly at Davis, he made ceramics based on vegetable images, but soon the human figure, and

Marilyn Levine, Canada, b. 1935. *Two-Tone Bag,* 1974. Stoneware. H.: 9 in. Gift of Howard and Gwen Laurie Smits. M.87.1.77.

Opposite:
Elaine Carhartt, United States, b. 1951. *Queen,* 1980. Ceramic and wood, painted with acrylic. H.: 53 in. Modern and Contemporary Art Council Young Talent Purchase Fund. M.82.65.

particularly the head, began to dominate his work. A trip to Paris in 1957, including a visit to Giacometti's studio, was of key importance to the young sculptor, and Modigliani, Indonesian aboriginal art, and the great heads from Easter Island also find echoes in his art. His elongated figures combine whimsy and frivolous humor with mock solemnity. *Hood,* 1985 (right), is typical of his mature sculpture. Built up by the coil method, it is larger than life-size, a woman's head mysteriously enclosed in a large cylindrical hood. Eyes peer through slits located far above where the eyes might be expected.

While VandenBerge's busts project a quiet, enigmatic seclusion, the solitary figures of Robert Brady (b. 1946) express vivid torment. Brady suffered a long and agonizing illness when he was sixteen, and there is little doubt that this early trauma affected his work. He studied ceramics at California College of Arts and Crafts and at Mills College before working with Arneson at Davis. His influence by Voulkos is tempered by an affinity for the work of Isamu Noguchi, especially the sculptor's "sensitivity to material and a sense that he has caressed and loved—made love to—the form, craft and material."[13] In the late 1970s Brady began a series of distorted masks, informed by the folk sculpture he admired during a stay in Mexico. Later, Septic River figures from New Guinea and Northwest Coast masks became important sources. *Aground,* 1985 (opposite), with its large bulbous head, barely supported by its emaciated body and leaning against a grid, wears an expression of alienation and bewilderment, reminding us of Friedrich Nietzsche's phrase "the eternal wounds of existence" and exemplifying the sculptural eloquence that can be achieved with clay.

Peter VandenBerge, Holland, active United States, b. 1935. *Hood,* 1985. Ceramic. H.: 36 in. Smits Ceramics Purchase Fund. AC1995.165.1.

Robert Brady, United States,
b. 1946. *Aground,* 1985. Ceramic,
painted. H.: 70 in. Smits
Ceramics Purchase Fund.
AC1998.59.1.1-.4.

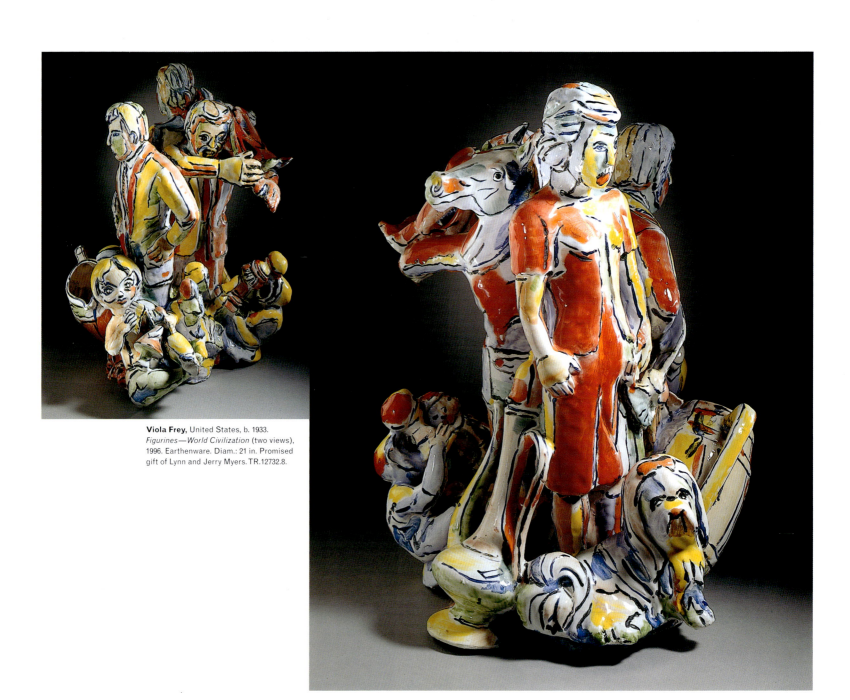

Viola Frey, United States, b. 1933.
Figurines—World Civilization (two views),
1996. Earthenware. Diam.: 21 in. Promised
gift of Lynn and Jerry Myers. TR.12732.8.

Another California artist who makes figurative clay sculpture is Brady's one-time teacher Viola Frey (b. 1933). Frey grew up on a vineyard in California's Central Valley and began working with clay at CCAC. For her graduate studies she enrolled at Tulane University in New Orleans, where Mark Rothko, a visiting artist in the winter of 1957, taught her about the emotional effects of color. Beginning in the 1970s Frey made small, colorful figures that, while uniquely her own, recall eighteenth-century porcelain figurines, Surrealist imagery, and Jean Dubuffet's grotesque Little Statues of Precarious Life. She has also produced a series of nonfunctional plates with glazed images that project from the flat surface. In *Crocker Series II,* 1979 (below right), her own two large hands, glazed dark blue, are presented prominently on each side of a black-suited man, an image of her friend the ceramist Howard Kottler, who frequently appears in her work.

In the 1980s Frey's figures increased markedly in scale, eventually reaching heights far beyond life-size. These figures are carefully constructed of separate ceramic sections, fired individually and then assembled into towering men and women. Strong colors—largely bright yellows and blues—enhance and enliven the surfaces. Typical is *Sky Blue Suit,* 1982 (p. 159), a solitary man with a perplexed expression, dressed in an ill-fitting business suit, standing as an iconic twentieth-century figure.

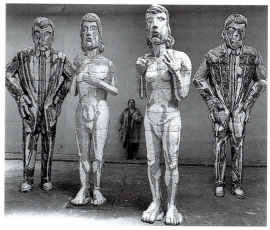

Viola Frey in her studio in Oakland, California, with her sculptures, 1991. Photograph by Christopher Irion, courtesy of Rena Bransten Gallery, San Francisco.

Viola Frey, United States, b. 1933. *Crocker Series II,* 1979. Ceramic, glazed. Diam.: 21 in. Gift of Howard and Gwen Laurie Smits. M.87.1.46.

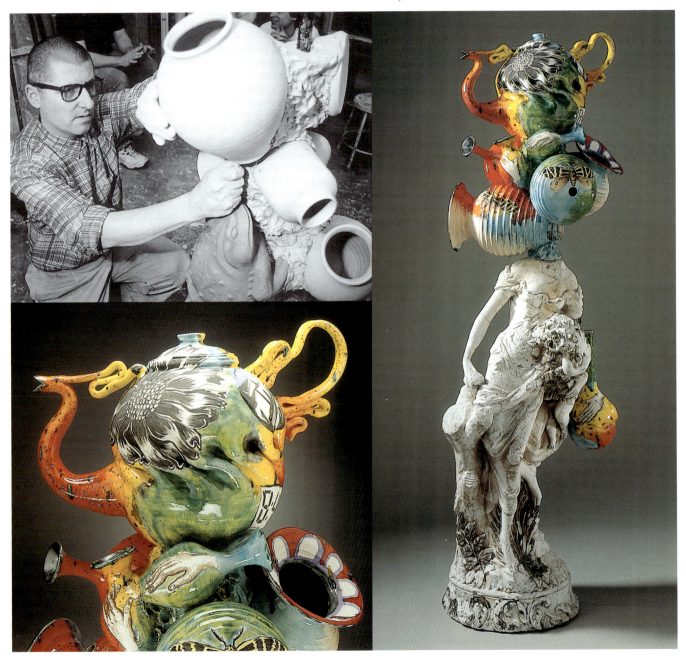

Michael Lucero in his studio in New York City, 1999. Photograph by John Jackson, courtesy of Dorothy Weiss Gallery, San Francisco.

Michael Lucero, United States, b. 1953. *Lady* (two views), 1998–99. White earthenware with found objects. H.: 53¾ in. Promised gift of Sonny and Gloria Kamm. TR.12633.1–.2.

Jack Earl, United States, b. 1934. *On no other day did the sun warm the grass as on that day* (front [left] and back), 1987. Ceramic with oil paint. H.: 35 in. Smits Ceramics Purchase Fund. AC1997.176.1.

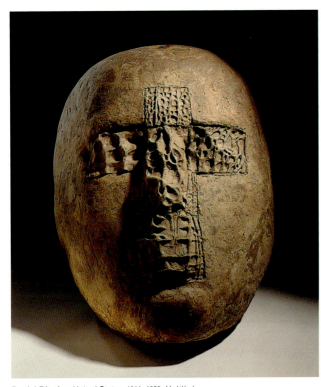

Daniel Rhodes, United States, 1911–1989. *Untitled (Head),* 1985. Stoneware, wood fired. H.: 21 in. Smits Ceramics Purchased Fund and gift of Shaw Guido Gallery. AC1998.267.1.

Although the recent surge in sculptural ceramics began in California, a number of artists working in different parts of the country and the world—Daniel Rhodes, Doug Jeck, Michael Lucero, Ruth Duckworth, Takako Araki, Akio Takamori, Phyllis Green, and Marek Cecula—have also followed impulses toward the figurative. Often but not always influenced by California ceramics, they address human, animal, or man-made forms, and their approaches are often startlingly different from one another as well as from the traditions from which their work emerged.

Daniel Rhodes (1911–1989) was born in Iowa and turned to figurative sculptural imagery late in his long and distinguished career as a ceramist, teacher, and author of influential technical publications on pottery. Originally trained as a painter at the Art Institute of Chicago and the Art Students League of New York, he began studying at the College of Ceramics at Alfred University in upstate New York and then taught on the Alfred faculty for many years. The ceramics school at Alfred is the oldest and most prestigious institution for the study of clay in this country. Initially set up primarily to train students for the ceramics industry, it was rather traditional until the 1950s, when, partly due to Rhodes's endeavors, it became more adventurous. Rhodes began to make vessels in which he combined clay with metal, wood, fiberglass, and bone. *Untitled (Head),* 1985 (left), is a late and exceptional work by the artist: a Christian cross embedded in a head of buff clay. As De Staebler did in his crucifix, Rhodes has avoided the trivial aspects of so much ecclesiastical work and rendered the cross as a meditative icon, anchored in earth.

Doug Jeck (b. 1963), working in Seattle, uses clay to form isolated human figures such as the pale ceramic *Projection,* 1977 (right). Like Auguste Rodin's *L'Homme qui marche* (1877/1905), which needs neither head nor arms for its wide, expansive stride, *Projection* is a human torso. But unlike Rodin's sculpture and stemming from a very different time and place, Jeck's nude male is a vulnerable figure with a haunting expression. The head with its inward gaze is superimposed on the beautifully modeled distorted torso, whose pose alludes to classical and Renaissance statues. The work is built of clay slabs that are made up of coils, and it stands without armature on its plinth, which is supported by a wooden base.

Michael Lucero was born in 1953 in California's San Joaquin Valley and educated in Seattle, and he spent a summer at Davis, where West Coast Funk artists such as Arneson, William T. Wiley, and Robert Hudson had an impact on him before he moved to live and work in New York in 1978. *Untitled (Dog),* 1982 (p. 181), belongs to a series of hanging shard sculptures he made in the late 1970s and early 1980s. To create these works, which defy the expectation that clay pieces should be integral wholes, Lucero strung numerous petals of fired clay, glazed in subtle colors, on multicolored strands of thin telephone wire and then hung them from the ceiling. The shards catch light and under certain conditions shimmer like dry leaves. Unlike Julian

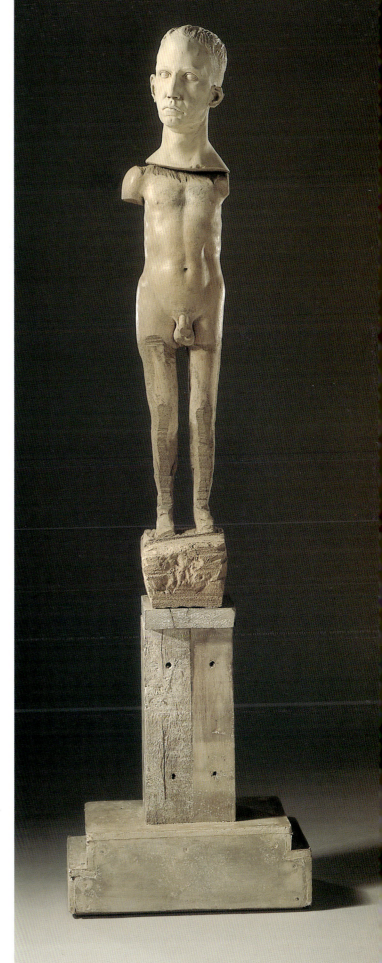

Doug Jeck, United States, b. 1963. *Projection,* 1997. Clay, wood, and drywall. H.: 62 in. Smits Ceramics Purchase Fund. AC1998.9.1.1–.2.

Schnabel's broken pottery pictures, which reflect violence, Lucero's fragile dog with its long legs, thin torso, and twisted and looped arms is a delicate spirit image. After this series of weightless sculptures, Lucero made a group of huge, disembodied clay heads with surfaces covered in paintings of idyllic landscapes, which refer to Brancusi's *Sleeping Muse.* In the 1990s he turned to anthropomorphic clay sculptures based on pre-Columbian and Native American sources. More recently he has been working on a series called Reclamations, chimerical assemblages of pieces found in antique shops or flea markets and then put back together in what appears to be a topsy-turvy manner and painted or glazed, giving a new and exuberant life to old kitsch (see p. 176).

Ruth Duckworth was born as Ruth Windmüller in Hamburg in 1919. She left Germany to escape Nazi persecution and went to England. Having known since she was a child that she wanted to be an artist, she attended art school in Liverpool. For a time she supported herself by making terra-cotta portraits and carving headstones for graveyards, work indebted to Henry Moore. After an early exhibition in London in 1955, she experimented in a great variety of materials and then decided to concentrate on clay. She went to the Hammersmith School of Art but found the instruction based on the purist potter Bernard Leach's theories too confining and transferred to the more liberal Central School of Art, where she later joined the faculty. Both her ceramic vessels and her reliefs became increasingly abstract, although forms of nature, such as the human body, stones, and seashells, seem to have inspired her.

In 1964 she was invited by the University of Chicago to teach at the Midway studios and she has remained in Illinois since that time. At Chicago she was commissioned to create a monumental wall sculpture, *Earth, Water and Sky,* 1967–68, for the Geophysical Science building. Since that time she has executed many additional mural commissions,

Left and above:
Two portraits of Ruth Duckworth, 1998. Photographs by Bill Mahin, courtesy of Thea Burger Associates, Geneva, Illinois.

Michael Lucero, United States, b. 1953.
Untitled (Dog), 1982. Ceramic, wire, and
metal. H.: 80 in. Smits Ceramics Purchase
Fund. AC1995.167.1.1–.4.

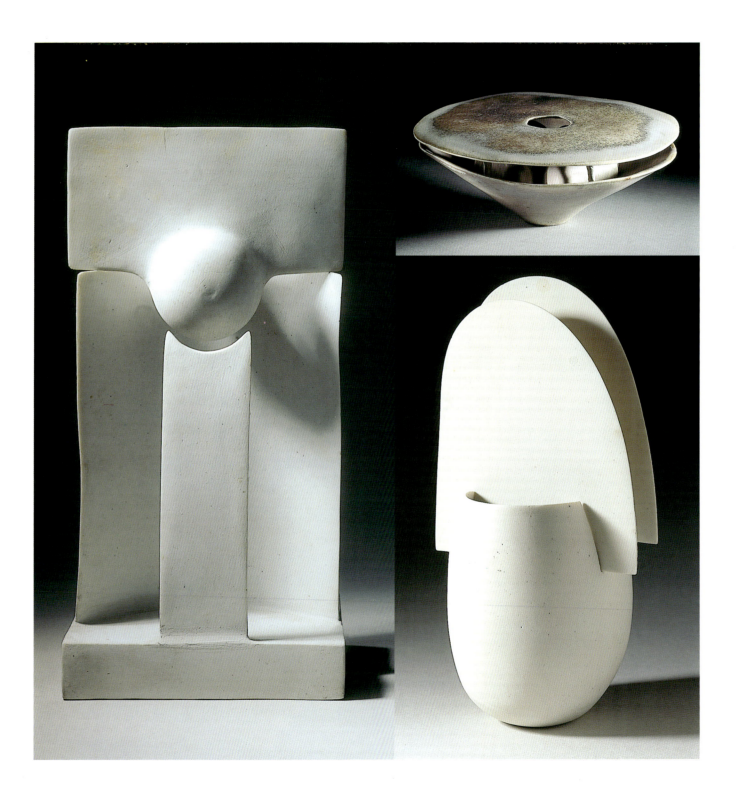

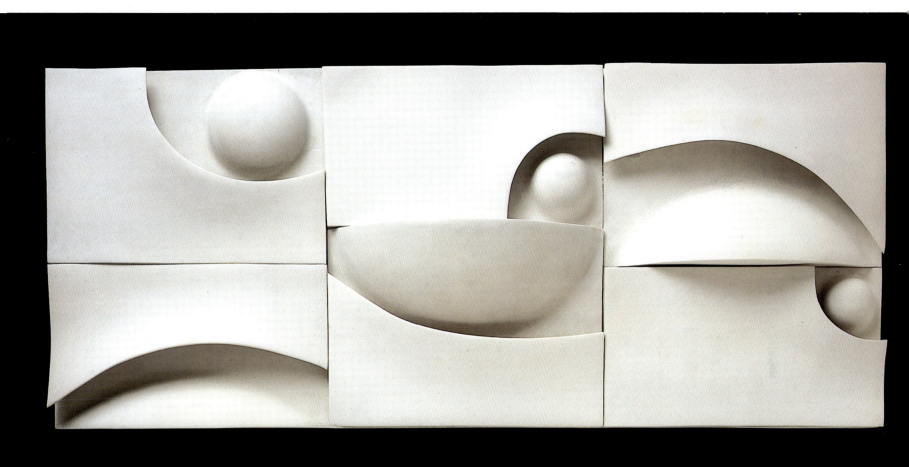

Ruth Duckworth, Germany, active
United States, b. 1919. *Untitled,* 1997.
Porcelain. W.: 56 in. Smits Ceramics
Purchase Fund. AC1998.28.1.

Opposite, counterclockwise from left:
Ruth Duckworth, Germany, active United States,
b. 1919.

Sculpture, 1988. Porcelain. H.: 12 in. Promised gift
of Lynn and Jerry Myers. TR.12732.6.1–.2.

Untitled (Blade Cup), 1994. Porcelain. H.: 8¾ in.
Smits Ceramics Purchase Fund. AC1995.167.2.1–.3.

Untitled, 1981. Porcelain. Diam.: 8½ in. Gift of
Howard and Gwen Laurie Smits. M.87.1.41a–b.

exhibited throughout the United States and in England, Germany, the Netherlands, Israel, Canada, and Japan. Her work is distinguished by a sensuous use of materials and simplicity of form. In *Sculpture,* 1988, and *Untitled,* 1997 (pp. 182 and 183), she develops the structural relationships of geometric forms in Oskar Schlemmer's Bauhaus sculptures—revisiting in her seventies, after many successful transitions, the art done in her native land in the early part of the twentieth century.

The ravaged but numinous Bibles by the Japanese ceramist Takako Araki (b. 1921) present another unique figurative aesthetic. For many years this artist, the atheist daughter of a Zen monk, has turned to the Judeo-Christian book of books as the theme of her work. She produces porcelain Bibles with patient and meticulous attention to detail, making thin sheets that she silkscreens with the sacred text and then tortures into illegibility. Araki has said that her work comments on "the various cruelties which have been committed for religion's sake throughout history and the false hopes religions have inspired."[14] Like the British artist John Latham, who destroyed books as his assault on the authority of language and the canon of knowledge, Araki renders scripture into corroded messages, endowing it with transcendent layers of meaning.

The younger Japanese artist Akio Takamori (b. 1950) has been making sensuous vessels marked by erotic narration. He writes, "I've been in love with the human figure since I was a child in Japan. My father's clinic was located in the red light district of our town; he was a dermatologist and it was always fascinating to watch the bodies of those coming in and out of the place."[15] He began his study of pottery in Tokyo, but after seeing California Funk sculpture, so totally different from the Japanese traditional discipline, he was eager to study in the United States. He eventually worked with the internationally known American ceramist Ken Ferguson at the Kansas City Art Institute. He later completed his education at the New York State College of Ceramics at Alfred University. Takamori now resides on Puget Sound and is a professor of ceramics at the University of Washington. There he continues to create playful, sensuous, and erotic porcelain and stoneware vessels that relate to Japanese Ukiyo-e woodblocks, especially the work of Utamaro, and Shinto fertility shrines with stone phalluses. They are also related to European traditions: Takamori mentions Brueghel and Picasso as early influences from Western art.[16]

Takako Araki, Japan, b. 1921. *Blue Bible,* 1987. Porcelain. W.: 10½ in. Gift of Howard and Gwen Laurie Smits. AC1995.97.1.

Akio Takamori, Japan, active United
States, b. 1950. *Under the Peach Tree*
(front [left] and back), 1994. Porcelain.
W.: 31 in. Promised gift of Lynn and Jerry
Myers. TR.12732.19.

His vessels explore polarities: Eastern/Western traditions, male/female, human/ animal, birth/death, and interior/exterior. Takamori begins a piece by making drawings on paper, which he uses as patterns to cut slabs of clay, one for the front and one for the back. After detailing and molding the flat slabs into lifelike contours, he fires the piece several times, using polychrome glazes to paint figures and animals, such as chickens or swans, on the smooth surfaces. He may magnify the curves and roundness of the female body to address men's desire for voluptuous women, as in *Thousand Years of Love,* 1988 (opposite), or address childbirth and its joy and conflicts, as in *Under the Peach Tree,* 1994 (p. 185).

Also discussing sexuality, but from a feminist or postfeminist point of view, is the work of Takamori's U.S. contemporary Phyllis Green (b. 1950). Green produces small mixed-media sculptures, with which she intends to "challenge the lingering modernist assumption that decoration and ornament, as feminine, are enemies of 'high art.'"[17] In 1994 she exhibited her installation *Turkish Bath,* a collection of abstract, eccentric, playful little sculptures made from a great variety of materials such as clay, velvet, leather, and feathers. As its title indicates, Green's work refers to J. A. D. Ingres's *Le Bain Turc* of 1862. Ingres's salon painting represents nude women, crowded together in their Oriental harem and assuming suggestive poses—a hymn to the glory of the female body as made available to the pleasure of the male voyeur-proprietor. Green's *Odalisque,* 1994 (p. 189), invokes the famous Ingres *Odalisque* of 1814, a painting of a reposing nude, descendent of all the great Venuses in Western art. In Ingres's version the icy colors and sharply delineated

Opposite:
Akio Takamori, Japan, active United States, b. 1950. *Thousand Years of Love,* 1988. Porcelain. W.: 28 1/4 in. Gift of Howard and Gwen Laurie Smits in honor of LACMA's twenty-fifth anniversary. M.90.82.53.

lines create a fascinating contrast to the nude's voluptuous pose, again inviting the male gaze. Green's piece is an abstract assemblage that imitates the reclining position of its namesake. On an overstuffed pillow lounges a construction of a large velvet bulb, a stoneware central element with dangerous-looking protuberances, and a long gray velvet tube ending in a yellow aperture—certainly open to many interpretations. It is a most intriguing sculpture, seductive in a very different way from past odalisques.

Marek Cecula (b. 1944) was born in Poland, studied sculpture in Cracow and ceramics in Israel, went to Brazil in 1962 as a designer of industrial porcelains, then moved to New York in 1977. He set up a studio and gallery, Contemporary Porcelain, in Soho, where he and his wife produced innovative porcelain dinnerware as well as nonfunctional vessels. In 1984 he began teaching ceramics at the Parsons School of Design, and he became head of the department in 1994. His sculpture, made of vitreous china, uses the techniques of industrial design and is associated with an international tendency

Phyllis Green in her studio in Santa Monica, California, 1999. Photograph by Ave Pildas, courtesy of Phyllis Green.

Top and detail, above:
Phyllis Green, United States,
b. 1950. *Odalisque,* 1994. Stoneware
and fabric. L.: 12 in. Gift of Connie
Tavel. AC1997.212.1.1–.2.

Right:
Marek Cecula, Poland, active
United States, b. 1944. *Untitled II,*
1996. Vitreous china on steel base.
Basin h.: 29 in. Base h.: 42⅝ in.
Smits Ceramics Purchase Fund.
AC1998.18.1.1–.6.

(sometimes referred to as the postcraft movement) that emphasizes a high-tech appearance. During a residence in the ceramics workshop in the town of 's-Hertogenbosch, Holland, he began his Scatology series. These sculptures have the stark white finish of commercial bathroom fixtures and are carefully displayed on stainless steel trays. Some of them resemble the lower parts of the human body as well as wash buckets. Cecula followed this group with the Hygiene series, of which *Untitled II,* 1996 (p. 189), is a fine example. Here he presents gleaming white basins, of porcelain that simulates vinyl, mounted on high steel stands in a row, like public wash-bowls, toilets, or urinals. A tubular discharge pipe dangles from each basin, evoking parts of human or animal organisms.

Back in 1919, Marcel Duchamp's urinal *Fountain,* 1913, submitted under the name R. Mutt, was banned from the Independents exhibition because, according to the hanging committee, it was nothing but a "piece of plain plumbing." In his historic response Duchamp, writing anonymously, proclaimed, "Whether Mr. Mutt with his own hands made the fountain or not has no importance. He *chose* it. He took an ordinary article of life, placed it there so that its useful significance disappeared under the new title and point of view—created a new thought for that object. As for plumbing, that is absurd. The only works of art America has given are her plumbing and her bridges."[18] Years later Arneson and Oldenburg made their own derisive sculptural comments on the toilet. Cecula's slick, clean, white bathroom fixtures have a similar satirical realism but a different effect. The emblems of clinical hygiene engender, perhaps inevitably in our era of AIDS, thoughts of disease and death.

The conceivable and actual possibilities of clay as an artistic medium seem to be without limits and are constantly extended. Almost two generations separate Voulkos's wildly Expressionist, roughly textured, gigantic stoneware sculptures from Cecula's basins, with their gleaming white industrial polish. And yet both artists, in their unique ways, crafted vessels made of clay. Their work, like the work of most of the artists in this exhibition, both incorporates and dissents from received tradition, advancing the potential of clay through new and surprising forms.

Peter Selz is professor emeritus of modern art at the University of California, Berkeley, and the founding director of the Berkeley Art Museum, University of California. He is the author of, among many other publications, *Beyond the Mainstream: Essays on Modern and Contemporary Art; Max Beckmann;* and *German Expressionist Painting.*

Opposite:
Beverly Mayeri, United States, b. 1944. *Sand Woman,* (two views) 1988. Buff clay, sand, and acrylics. H.: 17 in. Promised gift of Lynn and Jerry Myers. TR.12732.14.

Nancy Carman, United States, b. 1950. *Shackled,* 1989. White earthenware, glazed. H.: 18¼ in. Gift of Laurie and Eric Terhorst in memory of John Terhorst, courtesy of Helen Drutt, Philadelphia. AC1997.213.1.1–.3.

Notes

1   Karen Tsujimoto, "Peter Voulkos: The Wood-fired Works," in Rose Slivka and Karen Tsujimoto, *The Art of Peter Voulkos,* exh. cat. (Tokyo: Kodansha International in collaboration with Oakland Museum, 1995), 100.

2   Ibid., 102.

3   Jerome Tarshis, "Harold Paris: Emotions in Mixed Media," *Christian Science Monitor,* 14 December 1992, 16.

4   Stephen De Staebler, "Walls for Mem," in Peter Selz, *Harold Persico Paris* (San Francisco: Harcourts Modern and Contemporary Art, 1992), unpag.

5   Thomas Albright, *Art in the San Francisco Bay Area* (Berkeley: University of California Press, 1985), p. 138.

6   Richard Notkin quoted in John Natsoulas Gallery, ed., *30 Years of TB-9: A Tribute to Robert Arneson* (Davis, Calif.: John Natsoulas Gallery, 1991), 73.

7   Harold Paris, "Sweet Land of Funk," *Art in America* 55, no. 5 (March/April 1997): 97.

8   Peter Selz, *Funk,* exh. cat. (Berkeley, Calif.: University Art Museum, 1967).

9   Elaine Levin, *The History of American Ceramics* (New York: Harry N. Abrams, 1988), 230.

10   See Hilton Kramer, "Ceramic Sculpture and the Taste of California," *New York Times,* 20 December 1981, 31, 33.

11   Donald Kuspit, in *Robert Arneson,* exh. cat. (San Francisco: Fuller Goldeen Gallery; Benicia, Calif.: Studio AS, 1985), unpag.

12   Richard Shaw quoted in *30 Years of TB-9: A Tribute to Robert Arneson,* 62.

13   Robert Brady quoted in Thomas H. Garver, "Sleeping Creatures," in Janice T. Dreisbach, *Robert Brady: A Survey Exhibition,* exh. cat. (Sacramento, Calif.: Crocker Art Museum, 1989), 12.

14   Ronald A. Kuchta, *Takako Araki: Recent Work,* exh. cat. (Syracuse, N.Y.: Everson Museum of Art, 1988), unpag.

15   Akio Takamori with Peter Ferris, "Vessel Concepts," *Ceramics Monthly* 36, no. 2 (February 1988): 27.

16   Ibid.

17   Phyllis Green, artist's statement, November 1994.

18   Anonymous [Marcel Duchamp], "Comment," *Blind Man* 2 (May 1917), unpag.

Peter Shire, United
States, b. 1947. *Donald
(Scorpion Series),* 1996.
Earthenware. W.: 16 in.
Gift of Marvin and Judy
Zeidler. AC1999.40.

Better Living through Tea

Contemporary Artists Investigate the Teapot and Teacup

REBECCA NIEDERLANDER

And just as the Japanese amuse themselves by filling a porcelain bowl
with water and steeping in it little crumbs of paper which until then are
without character or form, but, the moment they become wet, stretch
themselves and bend, take on colour and distinctive shape, become
flowers or houses or people, permanent and recognizable, so in that
moment all the flowers in our garden and in M. Swann's park, and
the water-lilies on the Vivonne and the good folk of the village
and their little dwellings and the parish church and the whole
of Combray and of its surroundings, taking their proper
shapes and growing solid, sprang into being, town
and gardens alike, from my cup of tea.

Marcel Proust, *Swann's Way*

The teapot and its constant companion the teacup are steeped in cultural references. They may summon a Proustian nostalgia for a lost time, a cozy fireside domesticity, the Zen ideals of the Japanese tea ceremony, or the elaborate social codes of the nineteenth-century English tea. But as this essay sets out to suggest, these forms draw only a small portion of their allusions from their own rich past. Each pot and cup is an open world, inviting sophisticated discussions of art and life throughout history and into the coming millennium.

The origin of tea drinking is so lost in time that there are only legends to account for it: One story goes that the Chinese emperor Shen Cheng, c. 2737 B.C., discovered that boiling his drinking water prevented illness. One day, while he was traveling, the branch of a tea bush fell into his boiling pot, infusing the water with a bewitching aroma and flavor.[1] But no matter who first stumbled upon the rather implausible pleasure of water flavored with leaves, tea has played a significant role in the religion, philosophy, and politics of many cultures ever since. For centuries in China, it was drunk as a fine powder whisked with water in a bowl. The teapot itself was not invented until later, during the Ming dynasty, when the practice of brewing tea leaves became popular and the spouted oil and wine pots then in fashion were adapted for the purpose. Tea eventually moved to Japan, where the tea ceremony invented by Chinese Buddhist monks reached its spiritual apex. At the beginning of the seventeenth century, the drink arrived in Europe via Portuguese traders as an expensive import. In England it was first advertised as medicinal to allay the suspicions of the Puritans, who were quick to banish decadent foods. When it took hold as a social pleasure during the Restoration, it led to elaborate rituals and rules of etiquette. Still later, its heavy taxation was a catalyst for the American Revolution. With such varied domestic, social, and political connotations, it is not surprising that the accoutrements of its service—the teapot, the cup—have assumed so many styles and shapes.

The cups in LACMA's collection are drawn primarily from the gift of Betty M. Asher, who was renowned during her life for her devotion to this form—many artists created works specifically for her—and whose taste ran to adventurous and witty interpretations. Most of the teapots and additional cups that have been acquired through the Smits Collection and from private donors share this aesthetic. Therefore, LACMA's collection decidedly favors the nonfunctional vessel. Few of the pots or cups illustrated here were actually made for brewing or serving tea, to be judged for how smoothly they poured or how well they retained heat. Instead, each is designed to engage the viewer in an imaginative dialogue with the possibilities inherent in the vocabularies of these forms.

For centuries, function was seen as an essential element of the vessel; the trick was to make inventive shapes that worked. Then, in the 1920s, Kazimir Malevich, founder of the Suprematist movement, created a teapot that he claimed was not a working vessel at all but the *idea* of a teapot.[2] In this spirit, many postwar ceramic artists have relinquished the obligations of function entirely. The result is a group of intelligent, talkative, playful

Anthony Bennett, Great Britain, b. 1949.
Rock Cup and Saucer, 1984. Earthenware,
slip cast. H.: 8½ in. Gift of the Estate
of Betty M. Asher. AC1998.266.14.1–.2.

works of art that address each other and viewers across time and cultures, inviting us to an informal and lively tea party of the imagination. They have crossed the divide that separates the pot on the kitchen counter from the "useless" objet d'art behind a glass vitrine, but these objects don't snub their own utilitarian origins or the rituals in which their predecessors played such a central role. They wear their context proudly as they take their place among the modes of expression available to the contemporary artist.

Richard Notkin, one of the most accomplished sculptors in this mode, describes his approach in words that might apply to many of the artists represented here: "Although my work since 1983 has consisted almost entirely of teapots, I consider myself a sculptor with a strong commitment to social commentary. My chosen medium—the material I love to work with—is clay. The vessel is the primary 'canvas' for the ceramic artist, and my vessel of choice is the teapot, the most complex of vessels, consisting of body, handle, spout, lid, and knob. This allows me the widest latitude in juxtaposing the many images I use to set up my narrative pieces."[3] The cups and pots in LACMA's collection, although usually of a modest scale (particularly in comparison to the ambitious size of the works discussed in the preceding essays in this volume), contain big ideas, demanding—and rewarding—close attention.

Rock Cup and Saucer, 1984 (p. 197), by Anthony Bennett (b. 1949) is a good place to start looking, an example of how the postmodern cup rewards the attentive viewer with sophisticated comments on art and the human condition. The delicate, brightly colored, highly glazed cup, with its whimsically arched yellow handle, appears to be sinking into the hulking, roughly chiseled, polished brown rock form of its saucer. The disjunction between the two shapes does more than send up ideals of proportion and good design: The use of the "natural" rock as a foundation for the "man-made" cup forces us to recollect the fundamental relationship between these two objects. Rock is, after all, the source of the minerals in both clay and glaze; the cup is the rock reconstituted, here ambiguously balanced on its natural foundation, or at risk of being swallowed up by it. Bennett explains, "The history of ceramics is also the story of humans, and I have looked to the past to help me understand the present." He has described this cup as an allegory of contemporary humankind—we may be refined and sophisticated, but we're never far from our primitive origins.[4]

Like the cup, the teapot provides a compact venue for games of visual association about the tension between nature and artifice. *Midnight in the Garden of Eden,* 1999 (opposite), by Susan Thayer (b. 1957) presents a well-known story on its two sides: On one side, Adam and Eve stand on the cusp of eviction from their lushly artificial paradise, the serpent poised to strike; on the other, they are replaced by bare twigs. Intricately modeled reliefs surround the central, flat paintings: colorful greenery around the fringes, delicate butterflies perched on the handle, and a twisting, lurking snake. With her placement of the female nude on the front of the vessel, Thayer may be playing with the teapot's anthropomorphic associations. After all, we talk about the vessel in terms of the human form, naming its lip and body, measuring its shoulder in proportion to its neck, its waist to its foot. Most children learn the "I'm a little teapot" song and ever after-ward associate the handle and spout with human arms.

There is likely even more going on in this scene than meets the eye. The shell on the lid of Thayer's composition could be a reference to the legendary sixteenth-century French scholar and ceramic artist Bernard Palissy, who regarded the snail shell as the perfect design for a personal fortress, proposed it as the model for a utopian city, and used it frequently as a motif in his work.[5] Palissy's work may also have been on the mind of Susan Beiner (b. 1962) when she created *Red Shell Teapot,* 1997 (p. 200), almost completely burying the vessel in an architecture of shells. This pot is glazed in delicious, sun-licked colors, and its shape evokes a mythical, finned sea creature rising from the water. Beiner has said that the work is based on nostalgia for childhood experiences by the sea, and that the piling up of shells is a metaphor for the accumulation of memories in a life, some sweet, others painful.

Opposite:
Susan Thayer, United States, b. 1957. *Midnight in the Garden of Eden* (front and back),1999. Porcelain. H.: 14⅝ in. Promised gift of Jonathan Nelson. TR.12700.

Right:
Keisuke Mizuno, Japan, active United States, b. 1969. *Fruit Teapot,* 1999. Porcelain. W.: 8 in. Smits Ceramics Purchase Fund. TR.12638.1.1–.3.

Below, right:
Kathleen Royster, United States, b. 1958. *Spicey Harvest,* 1997–99. Porcelaineous stoneware. Teapot w.: 19 in. Creamer w.: 6½ in. Sugar bowl w.: 7½ in. Purchased with funds provided by Sonny and Gloria Kamm. TR.12647.1.1–.3.

Opposite:
Susan Beiner, United States, b. 1962. *Red Shell Teapot,* 1997. Porcelain, slip cast. W.: 12½ in. Gift of Jeff Guido and Friends. AC1999.108.1.1–.6 (TR.12670.1.1–.6).

Peter Shire, United States,
b. 1947. *Sunburst Accordion,*
1983. Earthenware, glazed.
H.: 16½ in. Promised gift of
Howard Farber. TR.12790.1.1–.2.

Attraction and repulsion is also the strategy of *Fruit Teapot,* 1999 (p. 201), by Keisuke Mizuno (b. 1969). This work lures the viewer with the jewel-like colors of what proves, upon closer inspection, to be a piece of realistically rendered overripe fruit being munched by alert-looking slugs. Mizuno has said that he is fascinated by the "beauty of the inseparable dependence and visual disparity between life and death." Humorously impractical, the pot is nestled in a leaf-shaped saucer of impossible fragility. Mizuno is clearly playing with the notion of forbidden fruit, the pomegranate of Hades as well as the apple of Eden, and possibly also the over-refinement of tempting luxury items that seem too precious to use or even touch. *Spicey Harvest,* 1997–99 (p. 201), by Kathleen Royster (b. 1958) also comments on contradictions in nature—the tender leaves protected by thorns—while nimbly unraveling centuries of tea ceremonies and traditions. A vessel designed to hurt seems the ultimate betrayal of hospitality.

Peter Shire (b. 1947), while pursuing a style different from Mizuno's, Beiner's, and Royster's, addresses the conflicts between form and function, good taste and bad taste, combining them in a yin-yang relationship the artist characterizes as "California Zen." He recollects an incident from his high-school days in the 1960s, when his mother told him he couldn't buy an outfit then in fashion because it would be in bad taste. The comment made him think about how people are defined by their likes and dislikes, and he decided that as an artist he wanted to master this temptation, presenting his dislikes positively and complaining about the things he loves. Of his teapot *Sunburst Accordion,* 1983 (opposite), he says that he was trying to amalgamate "all the bad taste I was ever confronted with."[6] The pale pinks, greens, and yellows are reminiscent of Southern California popular culture; the red handle with its spiky pattern is a tribute to the glass half-sunburst built above many doorways in Shire's childhood neighborhood of Echo Park. But the sunburst doubles as teeth, which makes the pot difficult to hold. Shire is a member of the postmodern Memphis design group, founded in Milan by Italian designer Ettore Sottsass, which invokes technology's positive and negative aspects in its sleek, strongly colored, architectural art.

Peter Shire holding clay circle and ball elements for teapots, 1983. Photograph © Gary Leonard, courtesy of Peter Shire.

Vessels have always provided a stage for storytelling—whether in a continuous frieze as on the Grecian urn immortalized by John Keats, on two flat sides, or simply in one expressive image that says it all. Narrative pots have existed at least since the ancient Greeks decorated their vessels with the accomplishments of their athletes. By combining painting and sculpture within a teapot or teacup, artists add excitement to a decorative object, engaging the viewer with the whole work.

Cindy Kolodziejski (b. 1962) started out as a painter, and her vessels have a refined, painterly surface that belies the energetic, highly physical, often almost brutal scenes they depict. *Sumo Wrestlers,* 1991 (right), turns the viewer into part of the audience at a sporting match; behind the wrestlers, other spectators return the viewer's gaze. In *A Day at the Races,* 1995 (opposite), Kolodziejski exploits the deep curve of her trophy cup to enhance the sense that the muzzled greyhounds are galloping toward the viewer around the track. On the reverse side, cheerleaders await the finish with contorted expressions.

Like Kolodziejski, Anne Kraus (b. 1956) trained as a painter, and she is known for painting the sides of her vessels with enigmatically captioned cartoons. *Adventures of Delphine: Delphine Carries a Cornerstone,* 1987 (p. 207), is an earthenware teapot painted with underglazes. Each side bears a central narrative cartouche surrounded by a gaily decorative

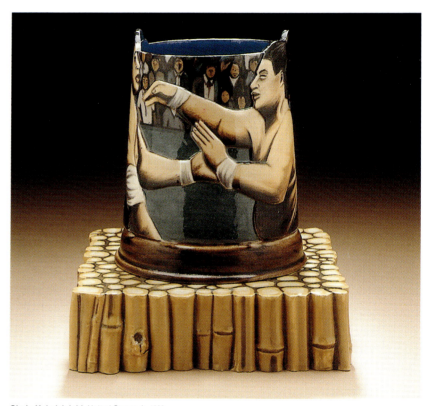

Cindy Kolodziejski, United States, b. 1962.
Sumo Wrestlers, 1991. Earthenware. H.: 4¾ in.
Gift of the Estate of Betty M. Asher.
AC1998.266.97.1–.2.

Cindy Kolodziejski, United States, b. 1962.
A Day at the Races (front [left] and back),
1995. Earthenware. H.: 15½ in. Smits
Ceramics Purchase Fund. AC1995.116.1.

The text on the vessel reads:

If is a stranger who struggles with this long and rambling good-bye, and yet I feel a sadness I cannot contain. I remember shadowy dreams of other lifetimes. And I realize I am a player on a magnificent game board but some of my pieces have rolled off an edge.

Left:
Anne Kraus, United States, b. 1956. *Ticket to Another World*, 1997. Whiteware. H.: 18 in. Smits Ceramics Purchase Fund. AC1997.39.1.1–.2.

Opposite:
Anne Kraus, United States, b. 1956. *Adventures of Delphine: Delphine Carries a Cornerstone*, 1987. Whiteware. H.: 11½ in. Gift of Howard and Gwen Laurie Smits. M.90.82.27a–b.

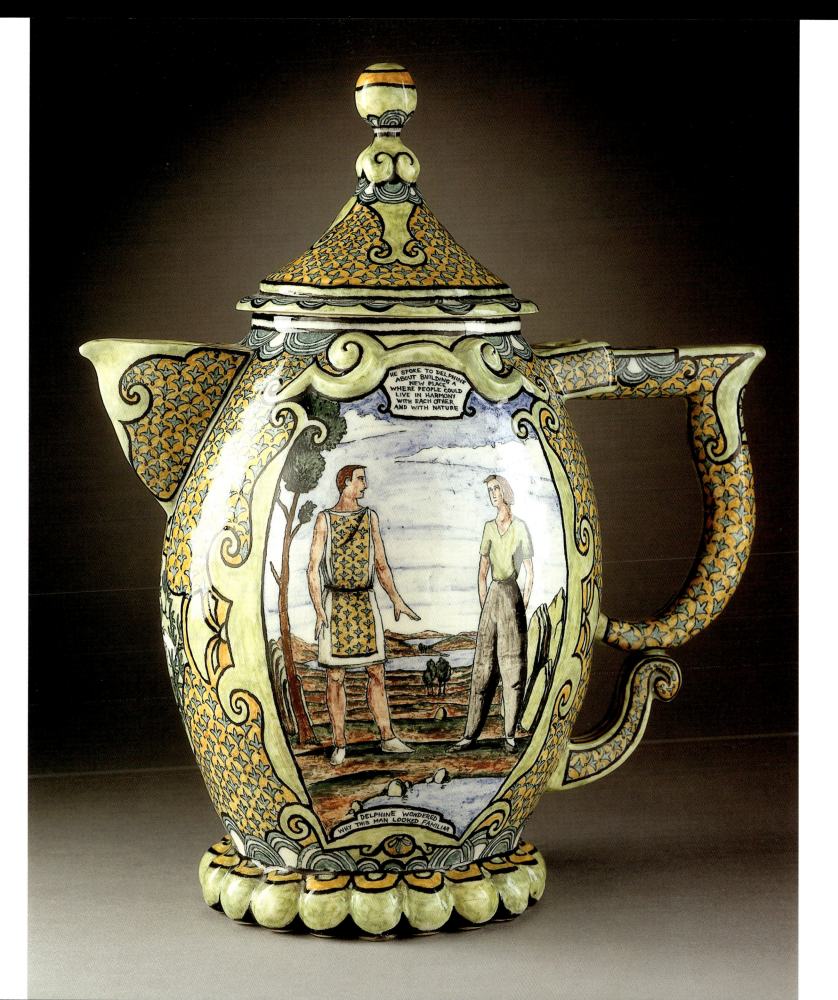

HE SPOKE TO DELPHINE
ABOUT BUILDING A
NEW PLACE
WHERE PEOPLE COULD
LIVE IN HARMONY
WITH EACH OTHER
AND WITH NATURE

DELPHINE WONDERED
WHY THIS MAN LOOKED FAMILIAR

motif of scrolls on a background of fleurs-de-lis. On one side, a woman in modern dress seems to converse with a male figure in a tunic (which echoes the fleur-de-lis pattern from the rest of the jar). The caption above the pair reads, "He spoke to Delphine about building a new place where people could live in harmony with each other and with nature." Beneath them is another caption: "Delphine wondered why this man looked so familiar." On the reverse, the man is seen setting off ahead over the hills, while Delphine follows him carrying a stone. The caption reads, "Together they carved a cornerstone and set forth." Some of Kraus's other vessels, such as *Ticket to Another World,* 1997 (p. 206), tell stories of similar poignant idealism, while others relate tales of idealism crushed by an unfortunate reality.

The Russian-born ceramic artist Sergei Isupov (b. 1963) uses narrative elements in a unique way, morphing human and animal figures, often in erotic postures, and decorative patterns together into odd new beings. His hand-built teapot *Two Planets,* 1999 (opposite), is at first glance a hideous, ambiguously amphibious creature dragging itself along on its belly. Its legs seem only half-evolved, with thorny white toenails growing, it seems, out of the bottoms of its reptilian feet. Its arms, however, are human. Its face resembles a frog's, with bright eyes and a disarmingly friendly expression. In contrast, the two colorless faces that rise from the creature's back are dour and grim, fixing each other with sidelong glances of unmistakable mistrust. The pot's small square lid, right in the center of the creature's head, is decorated with a severed hand with red, manicured nails. Naked figures appear elsewhere, tempting the viewer to pick up the beast and look for more. Although there is no linear narrative, a story is obviously being related: The creature could be interpreted as the embodiment of a romantic relationship, attempting to move forward despite its incomplete state of development; the two faces could be lovers trapped in this gross body and isolated from each other. The title seems to play on the pop culture idea that men and women are from different planets. Explaining his use of figurative elements in his work, Isupov has explained, "Decoration is nice, but you need [the] human for connection."[7]

Other artists tell stories in sculptural, rather than painterly, ways, often using their titles to bring the message home. *Mao Is Alive and Well, Swimming the Backstroke in the Yangtze,* 1975 (p. 210), by Gifford Myers (b. 1948) is a plain white coffee cup in which a cartoonish figure of Mao Tse-tung, cofounder and longtime chairman of the Chinese Communist party, is swimming—a reference to an obviously doctored photograph, released to the Western press in 1975, that supposedly showed the morning swim taken by the ailing chairman to prove his continuing strength to the people. Myers says that he strives to get "maximum effect through an economy of means."

Sergei Isupov, Russia, active United
States, b. 1963. *Two Planets* (two views),
1999. Porcelain. W.: 19½ in. Promised gift of
Sonny and Gloria Kamm. TR.1262.1.1.1–.2.

Study by Sergei Isupov.

Gifford Myers, United States,
b. 1948. *Mao Is Alive and Well,
Swimming the Backstroke in the
Yangtze,* 1975. Clay, glazed. H.: 3⅜ in.
Art Museum Council Fund.
M.83.230.40a–b.

This provocative approach was made particularly popular in the 1960s by the Funk movement
in Northern California (centered at the University of California, Davis), which sought to overcome
the stultification of the craft ideals then in fashion. Tired of the notion of the humble potter modestly
creating quiet works, the Funk artists made art that shouted—about politics, about sex, about
everything not acceptable to polite society. Robert Arneson (1930–1992), credited as the founder
of Funk, used himself as his subject matter, creating large-scale, witty,
often mocking self-portraits in clay. His palely glazed, handmade cup *Alice
Street House,* 1967 (opposite), is a small-scale and serene manifestation
of this autobiographical impulse, a commemoration of the place where
he lived, perhaps also a reference to eighteenth-century house-shaped
teapots. Arneson's student Chris Unterseher (b. 1943) created *Bauhaus, Faculty Residence,*
1973 (opposite), which resembles Arneson's piece in that it came out of a similar impulse
to document an important yet little-known world. In this case the world depicted is not autobiographical but historical. "Most of my ceramics document obscure historical events," he
writes. Most people know of some of the famous people who taught [at the Bauhaus], but
not many remember that they lived in identical experimental houses."

Robert Arneson, United States,
1930–1992. *Alice Street House,* 1967.
Ceramic. W.: 5⅞ in. Art Museum
Council Fund. M.83.230.4.

Chris Unterseher, United States,
b. 1943. *Bauhaus, Faculty Residence,*
1973. Ceramic. H.: 2⅜ in. Art
Museum Council Fund. M.83.230.78.

David Gilhooly, United States, b. 1943. *Pair of Beaver Cups,* 1973. Stoneware. Cup h.: 6¼ in. (left) and 6 in. Art Museum Council Fund. M.83.230.23a–b.

One of the primary impulses of Funk was to have fun. *Pair of Beaver Cups,* 1973 (above), by David Gilhooly (b. 1943), can be read as a send-up of the natural look and assumed naiveté of folk pottery. Gilhooly writes, "These were made when I was teaching a Saturday morning art class in Barrie, Ontario, where they only did stoneware, not my usual low-fired white earthenware. To amuse myself I started considering if I could hire beavers to do my work for me, so I started making clay branches and stumps and let them get to work." Gilhooly made *Coffee Break Selections,* 1989 (pp. 214 and 215), he writes, "to honor Betty Asher's fondness for the cup and what she did to promote every clay artist's obsession with making the most unusual and useless cup possible!" The box, designed and labeled like a chocolate sampler, is filled with small ceramic cups brimming over with Gilhooly's signature fake food: cookies and milk, noodles, cocoa with marshmallows— along with his ever-present group of merrily cavorting, splashing, wriggling frogs.

Ron Nagle (b. 1939), who studied ceramics with legendary teacher and sculptor Peter Voulkos at the University of California, Berkeley, has dedicated his career to the cup, and his work has freed a generation of artists to concentrate on this form. "It is not only the materials or processes that interest me," he explains, "but also the potential for intimacy inherent in the small object and the capacity of color to convey emotion."[8] His early work was distinctly Funk. Subsequent investigations led him to works like *Turkey Box Cup,* 1996 (opposite), which is displayed in a specially designed box. Nagle's box has no

Ron Nagle, United States, b. 1939.
Untitled (Turkey Box Cup), 1996. Porcelain
and mixed media. Box: 13 x 13 x 4 in. Cup
h.: 3 in. Smits Ceramics Purchase Fund.
AC1997.57.1.1–.2

lid, so the work can be mounted on the wall like a painting. The artist explains, "The imagery in this piece is from a Chinese martial arts book. In this case, I substituted a turkey for the bag of sand, which was in the original drawing." The whizzing turkey renders the delicate scene—with its connotations of the discipline and spirituality of the martial arts—comical.

Artists who work in clay at the turn of the millennium tend to be deeply aware of the traditions that preceded them, and they incorporate this knowledge into their work. They may focus on one era or style in ceramic history or mesh cultural references in a heady collage. Several contemporary artists use Yixing clay, both in a traditional spirit and with a postmodern edge. During the Ming and Qing dynasties, Chinese literati developed a taste for Yixing teapots, made of a richly colored and flexible clay found in the Kiangsu province. Yixing clay vitrifies well without a glaze and is so beautifully colored that it often doesn't need one. According to Garth Clark, the Yixing teapot became the focus of an unprecedented collaboration between scholars and potters: "The fascination of the literati with the teapot encouraged potters to push their aesthetic goals beyond merely meeting the simple design requirements of making a visually satisfying object and instead marked the point at which the teapot became a format for artistic self-expression."[9] These teapots, writes Vicki Halper, reflected the culture's "embrace of an intricate aesthetic that balanced natural tastefulness and simplicity (*qu*—the heart of the child), dramatic surprise (*qi*—shock or unbalance), formal orthodoxy, and meticulous craftsmanship."[10] Geo Lastomirsky (b. 1953), who

works in the Yixing tradition, has said that he attempts to bridge Eastern and Western means of expression and particularly to reconcile the disparate attitudes in the two cultures toward the role of the artist: "The Yixing potters I came to know are very distrustful of work that can, at best, be translated as being 'tricky.' Though they make some of the wildest functional wares the world is fortunate to receive, they are very honest in their making and brook no tolerance in the production of pots that glorify the maker rather than the traditions." His *Teapot #35*, 1997 (p. 216), is a powerful interpretation of Yixing traditions: a meticulously rendered, unglazed scene of rocks leaning against a tree stump, a miniaturized version of what looks like a massive petrified natural monument. "The monumentality I seek to build into my work is a reflection of places of excruciating beauty I have visited," he has written. "I started out wanting to be a monumental-scale artist. I finally figured out that everything is big when you're looking through a magnifying glass." It takes a second, third, or even a fourth glance at *Teapot #35* to discover the teapot within the craggy rock and tree.

Richard Notkin (b. 1953) adds his own artistic voice to this tradition. A former student of Arneson at the University of California, Davis, Notkin encountered Yixing ware after he graduated:

"I believe that the aesthetic impact of a work of art is not proportional to its size alone, but to its content.... At first attracted to the Yixing teapots' small scale, attention to detail, and imagery, I also became aware of their remarkable sense of proportion and composition, as well as their narrative qualities. The wide range of imagery—from purely geometric forms to totally organic studies of fruit and bundles of firewood or bamboo—is remarkable, demonstrating a phenomenal explosion of individual creativity.... The Yixing teapots are seemingly small and quiet at first encounter; closer inspection, and introspection, clearly reveals that these pieces are indeed powerful works of art.... Although I closely imitate the scale, formats, colors, and textures of the unglazed Yixing wares, my intention is to borrow from these formal qualities with honesty and a sense of homage. It is of utmost importance, however, that my pieces retain a totally separate cultural identity, that they reflect our contemporary civilization's imagery and speak of our society's current situation as we emerge from the twentieth century into the twenty-first."[11]

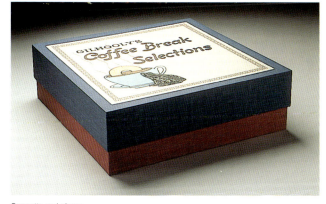

Opposite and above:
David Gilhooly, United States, b. 1943. *Coffee Break Selections,* 1989. Ceramic and mixed-media box. Box: 11 x 11 in. Cup h. ranges from 2½ to 3⅛ in. Gift of the Estate of Betty M. Asher. TR.12800.225.1–.10.

Geo Lastomirsky, United States, b. 1953. *Teapot #35,* 1997. Terra-cotta, unglazed, with terra sigillata and mixed media. W.: 12¼ in. Gift of Martha Fulton. AC1999.109.1.1–.2.

Richard Swanson, United States, b.1944. *Bird in Hand (Teapot),* 1997. Vitreous clay, polished. H.: 9 in. Promised gift of Ferrin Gallery. TR.12681.

Notkin's delicately crafted cups and pots trick the eye with their mimicry of natural or man-made forms, in which his deep concern with man's devastating effect on the environment is apparent: His *Cooling Towers Teapot (Variation #1)—Yixing Series,* 1983 (p. 218), has the shape of the towers at a nuclear plant, with human skulls on their lids, a form he had previously investigated in *Pyramidal Skull Teapot with Four Cube Skull Cups,* 1980 (p. 218). *Cup #2,* 1983, and *Cup #14,* 1984 (above left), both from the Tires series, seem to comment on the proliferation of discarded tires in our landscape, the ugly detritus of an industrialized society. Notkin writes, "All of the cups [from this series] are unique, and each walks a fine line between sculpture and functionality. But *Cup #14* goes over that line, as the functional capabilities are negated by the interior flanges of the five stacked tires, trapping any liquid—tea, perhaps—to the frustration of the sipper. Aesthetically, it is my favorite cup, despite its nonfunctional nature."

In the wake of the French Revolution, the French painter Jacques-Louis David declared the decorative arts an ugly reminder of the recently overthrown aristocracy and as such an unfit medium for true artists.[12] David believed that the lure of luxurious decorative vessels then in fashion among the wealthy and the bourgeoisie undermined the cause of the revolution (though even Sèvres produced wares with revolutionary symbols and political messages). Throughout the twentieth century, numerous artists from avant-garde movements have seen the opportunity in vessels to insinuate their messages into the homes of the people. LACMA's collection contains several examples, including work by Notkin, of cups with social messages. One

Richard Notkin, United States, b. 1948. *Cup #14* (left) and *Cup #2* from the Tires series, 1984 and 1983. Stoneware. H.: 3 in and 2½ in. Gift of the Estate of Betty M. Asher. AC1998.266.141 and AC1998.266.142.

of the earliest pieces in this vein is *Duke Edward Forever,* 1936 (right), by Michael Cardew (1901–1983), which protested the abdication of the duke because of his love for the twice-divorced American Wallis Simpson.[13] More recently, Scott Schoenherr (b. 1962) made *Golden Rhino,* 1996 (below right), as he has written, to mourn "the demise of the black rhino for its horn. Human ignorance has contributed to the large decrease of the rhino population as well as other animals and their environment. To express this conflict, I have used industrial symbols such as gears and dollar signs juxtaposed with mythical and folk symbols such as hands and ladders."

The replication of everyday objects is a rich field of endeavor for many contemporary artists. In the trompe l'oeil works of David Furman (b. 1945), distinctions between reality and fiction, between the real and the simulated, are explored in meticulously replicated every-day forms like pencils and erasers. Furman has described these pieces as "ersatz objects." As Carl H. Hertel wrote, "Mimetic work such as Furman's may be said to seek eternity and is classically attuned to an absolute grammar wherein signs are, dare we say, freeze-dried— Platonic aspirants to what [Michel] Foucault refers to as the *Taxinomia universalis.*"[14] Just

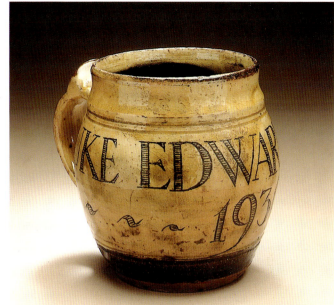

Michael Cardew, Great Britain, 1901–1983. *Duke Edward Forever,* 1936. Earthenware. H.: 6 in. Gift of Betty M. Asher in honor of LACMA's twenty-fifth anniversary. M.91.121.

Opposite:
Richard Notkin, United States, b. 1948.

Top:
Cooling Towers Teapot (Variation #1)—the Yixing series, 1983. Colored porcelain. H.: 9 in. Gift of Howard and Gwen Laurie Smits. M.87.1.118a–b.

Bottom:
Pyramidal Skull Teapot with Four Cube Skull Cups, 1980. Porcelain, glazed. Teapot w.: 9 in. Cup h.: 2¾ in. each. Gift of Howard and Gwen Laurie Smits. M.87.1.112a,b; M.87.1.113–.116.

Scott Schoenherr, United States, b. 1962. *Golden Rhino,* 1996. Whiteware. H.: 13¼ in. Howard Kottler Testamentary Trust. AC1996.43.2.1–.3.

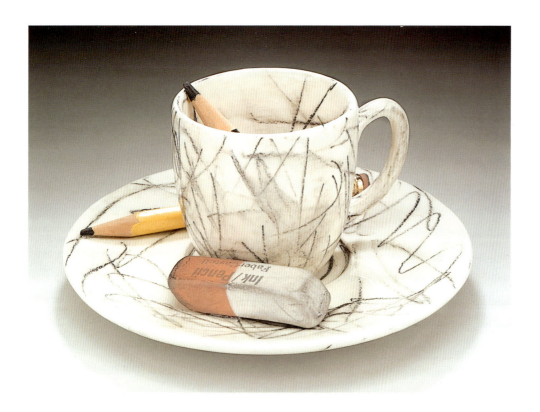

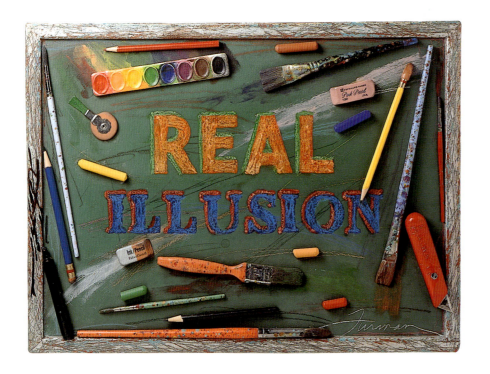

David Furman, United States, b. 1945.

Top:
Faber Castell Cup (Demi), 1987. Ceramic, underglazed and glazed. H.: 2¼ in. Gift of Estate of Betty M. Asher. AC1998.266.63.

Left:
Real Illusion, 1994. Ceramic, underglazed, glazed, and painted. W.: 23¼ in. Gift of Herbert and Jean Bloch. TR.12727.1.

as a stuffed mouse or sparrow might offer
an unanticipated discovery of beauty—the
absolute, eternal beauty of a Platonic ideal—
Furman's fastidious renderings reveal an
unexpected grace in the line and texture of
an object as simple as a pencil (opposite).

Other artists trick the eye in different
ways. *Le Souci de Soi* (The Care for the Self),
1984 (p. 222), is a set of puzzle-like dishes by
Canadian artist Paul Mathieu (b. 1954). Their
design appears to be abstract and random, until
they are viewed from above and stacked so that
the lines come together just right. Suddenly
they present a picture: "a self-portrait superimposed on a male nude, with a hand, on a
background of yellow roses." The work is part of
a series of four, based, according to the artist,
on the four books of Foucault's *The History of
Sexuality.* (*Le Souci de Soi* is the third book in
the series.) Mathieu is part of an informal group
of Montreal-based artists, including Léopold
L. Foulem (b. 1945; his work is represented on
p. 233), whose terrain is "the epistemology of
ceramics and pottery."[15] Taking the view that
ceramics exists on the periphery of current
modes of art critical discourse, according to
Bruce Hugh Russell, these artists "have sought
to lay bare the irrelevance of the outmoded
hierarchies of high and low, fine and decorative,
in sculpture. In embracing a medium denigrated
as effete and superficial these artists have
found a vehicle to explore their own social
status as gay men and as artists in contestation
of received social roles."[16] Mathieu infuses his

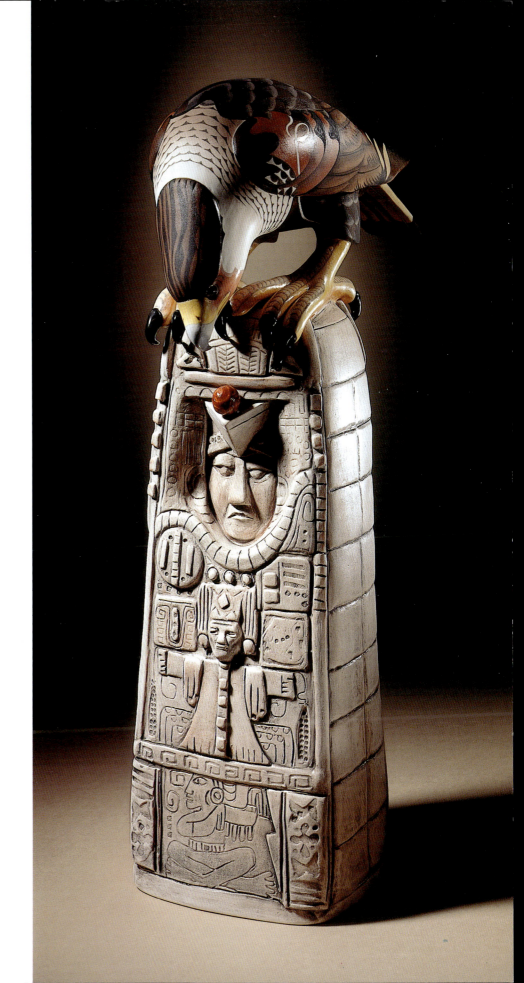

Annette Corcoron, United
States, b. 1930. *Cara Cara,* 1998.
Porcelain. H.: 17 ½ in. (44.5 cm).
Gift of Dorothy Weiss Gallery.
TR.12752.1.1–.2.

Paul Mathieu, Canada, active United States and Canada, b. 1954. *Le Souci de Soi (The Care for the Self),* 1984, two views, stacked (right) and traditionally arranged (below). Porcelain. H. (stacked): 7 ½ in. Gift of Howard and Gwen Laurie Smits in honor of LACMA's twenty-fifth anniversary. M.90.82.38a–f.

works with philosophy, sexuality, and art history in sophisticated ways that confound the lingering expectation that teapots and cups ought to be plainspoken. *The Fold on Differance,* 1988 (right), is another stack of saucers and a cup that uses visual trickery: Seen from above, the three pieces look like a flat painting of a teapot, with the phrase "This is not a teapot" painted underneath. This work, Mathieu explains, "is obviously based on René Magritte's famous painting *The Treachery of Images* [with its famous slogan *Ceci n'est pas un pipe* (This is not a pipe)]." "The fold on differance" is from a French-Canadian phrase that, according to Mathieu, means "I really couldn't care less." "If 'this is not a teapot,'" he asks of this piece, "is it anymore a cup?"

Others who play with craft and art conventions include Lucian Pompili (b. 1942) and Edie Ellis-Brown (b. 1937). Pompili's *East,* 1997 (p. 224), is a collection of pre-molded pieces salvaged from commercial slip mold shops. Similarly, Ellis-Brown, in the narrative sand cup series that includes *Cowboy with Pony,* 1990 (p. 224), combines existing or nonart materials such as plastic figurines and ceramic cups and covers them with glue and sand. Taking cues from Joseph Cornell's combinations of found materials and Meret Oppenheim's fur-lined teacup or her *Souvenir du "Déjeuner en Fourrure" (Souvenir of "Breakfast in Fur"),* 1936/1972, Ellis-Brown attempts to turn the functional into something meant to be contemplated, creating magical worlds in which miniature and human-scale objects come into new relationships. A similar impulse to create teapots that discuss not craft traditions but teapots themselves—a postmodern

Paul Mathieu, Canada, active United States and Canada, b. 1954. *The Fold on Differance,* 1988. Ceramic. H. (stacked): 5½ in. Gift of the Estate of Betty M. Asher. AC1998.266.125.1–.3.

Meret Oppenheim, Switzerland, 1913–1985. *Souvenir du "Déjeuner en Fourrure" (Souvenir of "Breakfast in Fur"),* original 1936, realized in 1972. Mixed media. W.: 7¾ in. Gift of the Estate of Betty M. Asher. TR12800.1.1.

Lucian Pompili, United States,
b. 1942. *East,* 1997. Porcelain
with iron shavings. H.: 14½ in.
Gift of Lucian Pompili in honor
of Rose Pompili. TR.12706.1.1–.2.

Edie Ellis-Brown, United States, b. 1937.
Cowboy with Pony, from Narrative Figures
series, 1990. Ceramic cup with plastic
figures and sand. H.: 4⅛ in. Gift of the
Estate of Betty M. Asher. AC1998.266.43.

self-referentiality—appears in works such as *Teapot and Stand,* 1988 (right), by James Lawton (b. 1954), where teaspoons and cups float across the surface of the pot, and *Tea Tower,* 1998 (below right), by Joan Takayama-Ogawa (b. 1955), a highly decorated stack of teapots painted with teapots. Takayama-Ogawa expresses the unique perspective on the Japanese tea ceremony of a Sensei, or third-generation Japanese American.[17]

One of the most popular themes in this genre seems to be deconstruction of the physical form of the pot and cup—a practice that harks back to the beginning of the century, when Lucio Fontana (1899–1968), the Argentina-born, Italian-educated painter, theorized that "the aesthetics of organic motion had replaced the outmoded aesthetics of fixed forms."[18] He explored this idea in his unpainted or minimally painted, sliced, and pierced canvases, and in his Spatial Concept Vases. In *Untitled,* 1972 (p. 226), by Robert Arneson, the holes punched in the sides of the cup and saucer seem to have been rolled into balls and placed inside, a thought-provoking comment on the ordinary relationship of liquid and solid in a cup. In *Teapot Diptych (Moonrise and Jackhammer),* 1984 (p. 226), Philip Cornelius (b. 1934) cut triangles in one of the vessel walls and folded them back to create a sieve-like look. *Wire Teacup and Saucer,* 1990 (p. 226), by Patrick Hilferty (b. 1958), reveals a skeletal structure

Top:
James Lawton, United States, b. 1954. *Teapot and Stand,* 1983. Earthenware. H.: 7 in. Gift of Howard and Gwen Laurie Smits. M.87.1.72a–c.

Above:
Joan Takayama-Ogawa, United States, b. 1955. *Tea Tower,* 1998. Whiteware. H.: 14 in. Promised gift of Ferrin Gallery. TR.12649.1.1–.2.

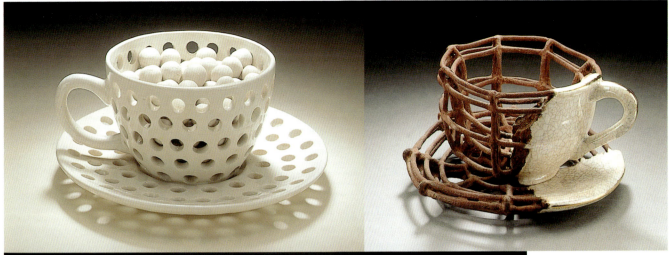

Above, left:
Robert Arneson, United States,
1930–1992. *Untitled,* 1972. Porcelain.
W.: 5¹³⁄₁₆ in. Art Museum Council
Fund. M.83.230.6.

Above, right:
Patrick Hilferty, United States,
b. 1958. *Wire Teacup and Saucer,*
1990. Stoneware. H.: 3¹⁄₈ in. Gift
of the Estate of Betty M. Asher.
AC1998.266.76.

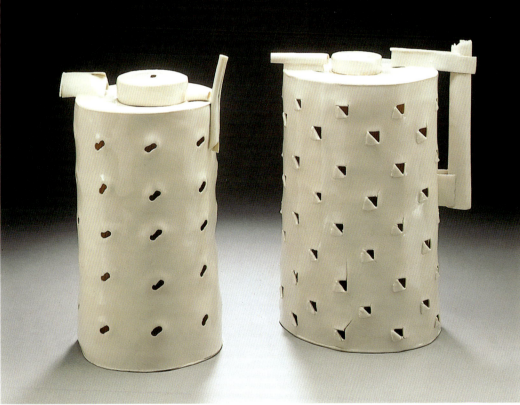

Philip Cornelius, United
States, b. 1934. *Teapot Diptych
(Moonrise and Jackhammer),*
1984. Porcelain. H.: *Moonrise*
(left): 11 in.; *Jackhammer:* 10½ in.
Smits Ceramics Purchase Fund.
AC1997.56.1.1–.4.

Left:
Lucian Pompili, United States, b. 1942.
Alice's Teacup, 1972. Porcelain. H.: 3⅞ in.
Art Museum Council Fund. M.83.230.53.

Far left:
Irv Tepper, United States, b. 1947. *Cup
and Saucer,* 1984. Porcelain. H.: 6⅝ in.
Gift of Jeanne and Dan Fauci.
AC1999.41.1.1–.2.

Paul Dresang, United States, b. 1948. *Teapot,*
1988. Porcelain. Width: 18 in. Promised gift of
Lynn and Jerry Myers. TR.12732.5.

under the white enamel, almost like a cut-away or medical diagram. He writes, of the series of which this cup is part, "I had been making teapots that attempted to challenge some ceramic conventions. Briefly, this involved reconceiving the ceramic vessel in terms of a structure that could describe, but not contain, in any literal sense, a volume. Such a teapot would be contradictory: It could not perform any of the functions of a teapot with the exception of identifying itself as a teapot. In addition, a teapot that utilized an architecturally derived skeletal structure could, I felt, play with the convention of a vessel as a metaphor for the body."

Similar concerns can be found in the work of Raymon Elozua (b. 1947), who was a student of ceramic sculptor Ruth Duckworth at the University of Chicago. Of *Reconstructed Teapot and Cup #4,* 1987 (below), he writes, "The vessel has often been described as a metaphor for the human body. This work was concerned with the interior architecture of a skeleton, which supported the surface or skin of a vessel."

Raymon Elozua, Germany, active United States. *Reconstructed Teapot and Cup #4,* 1987. Terra-cotta, glazed, and metal. Teapot h.: 25 in. Cup h.: 6¼ in. Gift of Allan Chasanoff. AC1993.93.1.1–.2.

Andrew Lord, Great Britain, active United States, b. 1950. *Two Patterned Cups,* 1985. Ceramic. H.: 4¼ in. (left) and 4⅞ in. Gift of the Estate of Betty M. Asher. AC1998.266.106 and AC1998.266.107

Background:
Study by Andrew Lord.

Like Elozua's tea set, *Two Patterned Cups,* 1985 (p. 229), by Andrew Lord (b. 1950), shows a debt to Cubism. Critic Christopher Knight has called Lord's vessel sculptures "pictures that have been pushed, pulled, coaxed, and cajoled into volumetric space," adding that these works "make a direct assault on a central piety of artistic practice: They're about the chosen motifs and about the process of seeing these motifs—but they're about *already having seen* the motifs as well."[19] The work of Lord's fellow English artist Linda Gunn-Russell (b. 1953) and the Hungarian-born artist Nicholas Homoky (b. 1950) also explores the process of looking at vessels. A Gunn-Russell vessel may appear at first glance like a tall, rounded vase but in fact does not have the same volume as a functional object one might set on a table. In this way, Gunn-Russell's flattened, slab-built *Teapot,* 1985 (opposite), and Homoky's *White Teapot,* 1980, and *Teacup (Cup with Cups),* 1981 (both p. 232), for example, question how we interpret space visually.

Along with Gunn-Russell, Henry Pim (b. 1947), and Sara Radstone (b. 1955), Angus Suttie (1946–1993) was a student at the Camberwell School of Arts and Crafts in England in the late 1970s.[20] Suttie gave his hand-built *Untitled Cup,* 1982 (right), a highly finished quality. In contrast to other artists of his generation who pursued art-historical or autobiographical themes in their work, Suttie stressed an intuitive process in the creation of his free-form objects, expecting viewers to find humor in his peculiar warping of traditional forms.

Many ceramic artists incorporate so many references in small spaces that unpacking their resonances could take volumes. Craig Owens has written that "allegorical imagery

Angus Suttie, Scotland, 1946–1993. *Untitled Cup,* 1982. Earthenware. H.: 5 in. Gift of Dan Fauci. AC1995.82.1.

Linda Gunn-Russell, Great
Britain, b. 1953. *Teapot,* 1985.
Earthenware. H.: 12 in. D.: 1½ in.
Gift of Howard and Gwen Laurie
Smits. M.87.1.52.

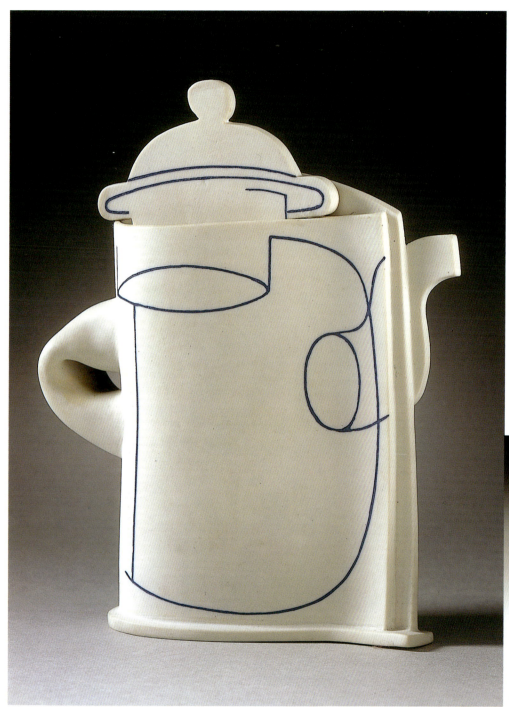

Nicholas Homoky, Hungary, active England, b. 1950.

Left:
White Teapot, 1980. Porcelain with inlaid Mason Stain slip. H.: 7⅛ in. Gift of Howard and Gwen Laurie Smits. M.87.1.64a, b.

Below:
Teacup (Cup with Cups), 1981. Porcelain with inlaid Mason Stain slip. H.: 3⅝ in. Gift of the Estate of Betty M. Asher. AC1998.266.80.

is appropriated imagery; the allegorist does not invent images but confiscates them. He lays claim to the culturally significant, poses as its interpreter. And in his hands the image becomes something other (*allos*=other and *agoreuei*=to speak).... The allegorical meaning supplants an antecedent one; it is a supplement. This is why allegory is condemned, but it is also the source of its theoretical significance."[21] According to Walter Benjamin, it is the practice of allegory to pile up fragments.[22] Léopold L. Foulem's *Blue-and-White Teapot with Oriental Landscapes,* 1996 (below), unites a found object, in this case a European silver teapot holder, with the form of a Chinese teapot that bears a painted scene in blue and white. Chinese export ware was often decorated in blue and white, and European potters did their best to imitate it in the eighteenth and nineteenth centuries. Rather than work within this traditional narrative style, however, Foulem chooses to recontextualize these wares within a European vernacular, quoting the stylistic appropriations of Chinese wares common in eighteenth-century European ceramics.

Léopold L. Foulem, Canada, b. 1945. *Blue-and-White Teapot with Oriental Landscapes,* 1996. Ceramic with found objects. H.: 12 in. Smits Ceramics Purchase Fund. AC1999.48.21–.3.

Michael Gross, United States, b. 1953. *Teapot,* 1988. Earthenware. H.: 12 in. Promised gift of Lynn and Jerry Myers. TR.12732.9.1–.2.

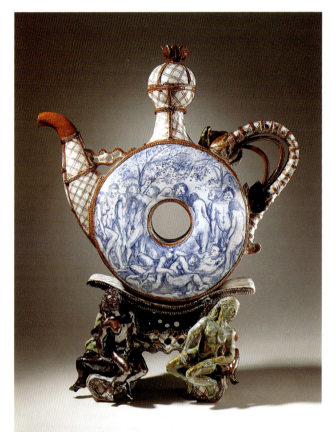

The large *Teapot,* 1990 (left; see also p. 194) by Ann Agee (b. 1959) is a complex confection that amalgamates several motifs and styles from centuries past, including colorfully painted classical mythological figures and cobalt stain drawing reminiscent of cozy Staffordshire and Delft ware. The symbol of seventeenth-century Holland—that country's so-called golden era—was the tulip. Every middle-class garden brimmed with these flowers, and the factories at Delft turned out complex multimouthed vases to hold them.[23] Nimbly incorporating references to such Delft vases and to Chinese blue-and-white ware, heavy patterning, and well-sculpted figurines, Agee puts an elegant, original bow on ceramic history.

Adrian Saxe (b. 1943) is the ultimate accumulator, carefully organizing and storing fragments of pop culture, such as plastic toys and jewelry, for years until the perfect construct presents itself. In *Untitled Ewer (Chou),* 1991 (opposite), Saxe uses such elements in a playful exchange with concepts taken from eighteenth-century nature studies. "Historically, the pursuit of scientific inquiry has provided the impulse to organize nature," Saxe says. "Age of Reason scientists would investigate an object, organize it into an image bank, combine, idealize, redraw, idealize again, then adapt those idealized objects into highly stylized ones not found in nature, often in an effort to own and dominate that which was formerly intimidating."[24] Saxe, on the other hand, incorporates

Above, left:
Ann Agee, United States, b. 1959. *Teapot* (back), 1990. Earthenware, glazed. H.: 26 in. Promised gift of Lynn and Jerry Myers. TR.12732.1.1–.3. For front view see p. 194.

Left:
Liza Lou, United States, b. 1969. *Cup and Saucer,* 1992. Mixed media. H.: 3¼ in. Gift of the Estate of Betty M. Asher. AC1998.266.108.1–.2.

Opposite:
Adrian Saxe, United States, b. 1943. *Untitled Ewer (Chou),* 1991. Porcelain with lustres and blue sapphire rhinstones. H.: 10 in. Promised gift of Lynn and Jerry Myers. TR.12732.

Adrian Saxe in his studio, 1992.
Photograph © Anthony Cuñha.

Porntip Sangvanich, Thailand,
active United States, b. 1959.
Butterscotch Teapot and Teacup,
1999. Whiteware. Teapot w.: 9⅜ in.
Cup w.: 5⅜ in. Promised gift of
Sonny and Gloria Kamm (teapot)
and gift of Corinth Ceramics Studio
(cup). TR.12730.1.1–.2 and TR.12731.

Carmen Collell, Spain, b. 1951.
Teapot, Two Teacups, and Saucers,
1984. Earthenware, burnished. Teapot
w.: 10 in. Cup h.: 4¾ in. each. Gift
of Howard and Gwen Laurie Smits.
M.87.1.24a–b; M.87.1.26a–b and
M.87.1.25a–b.

nature into this piece, such as a real cabbage, which he cast in porcelain and then modified. His art has been linked critically to Baroque and Rococo ornament, but he calls this interpretation an obfuscation of his true intent, noting that the "transposition of intellectual inquiry from one mode to another (a reinventing of traditional form) has added value for each new generation, and depends on insights from each generation's successor."[25]

Finally, the notion of accumulation also seems pertinent to the work of Liza Lou (b. 1969), who rose to acclaim with *Kitchen* (1991–95) and *Back Yard* (1995–97), two room-size installation sculptures incorporating found and made objects covered entirely in glass beads. Lou wants her work to express her "fastidious take on every square inch of life."[26] She financed *Kitchen* by selling several of its elements, including *Teacup and Saucer,* 1993 (p. 234), along the way. She has said that this work comes from the same impulse that drove William Blake to write, "To see a world in a grain of sand/ And a heaven in a single wild flower/Hold infinity in the palm of your hand/And eternity in an hour."

This impulse—to compress vast worlds into small objects—has clearly motivated all the artists here to layer dense histories and issues of art and culture onto their adventurous and intellectually challenging pieces. Each of these vessels provides as evocative a voyage through time as Proust's cup. Style is an expression of the philosophies of a culture, and icons of the dominant style describe best what the culture values. These teacups and teapots can show us who we have been, who we are today, and who we may expect to be tomorrow.

Rebecca Niederlander assisted with the exhibition *Color and Fire: Defining Moments in Studio Ceramics, 1950–2000.* She holds an MFA from the University of California, Los Angeles, a BFA in ceramics from California College of Arts and Crafts, and a BA in journalism from Southeast Missouri State University. Her art has been exhibited nationally and featured in numerous publications, including the textbooks *Hands in Clay* and *Make It in Clay.*

Keiko Fukazawa, Japan, b. 1955. *Kei/View,* 1987. White earthenware, glazed and lustered. W.: 22½ in. Gift of Howard and Gwen Laurie Smits in honor of LACMA's twenty-fifth anniversary. M.90.82.25a–d.

Notes

1 See Garth Clark, *The Eccentric Teapot: Four Hundred Years of Invention* (New York: Abbeville, 1989), 25. Clark's book, which contains excellent brief histories of tea, its rituals, and the teapot form, is a primary source for the information in this summary. See also his *The Book of Cups* (New York: Abbeville, 1990); Rand Castile, *The Way of Tea* (New York: Weatherhill, 1971); Patricia Graham, *Tea of the Sages: The Art of Sencha* (Honolulu: University of Hawaii Press, 1998); Janet Street-Porter and Tim Street-Porter, *The British Teapot* (London: Angus and Robertson Publishers with the Tea House, 1985); and Sen Soshitsu XV, *The Japanese Way of Tea: From Its Origins in China to Sen Rikyu* (Honolulu: University of Hawaii Press, 1998).

2 See Clark, *The Eccentric Teapot,* 57.

3 In preparation for this volume, during the spring and summer of 1999, artists were invited to submit statements about their work, goals, and careers, as well as studies and preparatory sketches. Their generous responses gave rise to a valuable collection of resources on this contemporary generation and its art. Unless otherwise noted, quotations attributed to the artists are taken from their submissions.

4 Conversation with Anthony Bennett, 16 August 1999.

5 Gaston Bachelard, *The Poetics of Space* (Boston: Beacon Press, 1994), 128.

6 Conversation with Peter Shire, 8 December 1999.

7 Sergei Isupov, interview by Karen S. Chambers, *American Craft* (February/March 1999): 63.

8 Ron Nagle quoted in "Up Front," *Ceramics Monthly* 46, no. 8 (October 1998): 14.

9 Garth Clark, *The Eccentric Teapot,* 52.

10 Vicki Halper, *Strong Tea: Richard Notkin and the Yixing Tradition* (Seattle: Seattle Art Museum, 1990), 1–2.

11 Richard Notkin, "Artist's Statement on the 'Yixing Series,'" 1985.

12 Arthur Danto, *Embodied Meanings: Critical Essays and Aesthetic Meditations* (New York: Farrar, Straus, Giroux, 1994), 301.

13 Clark, *The Book of Cups,* 58.

14 Carl H. Hertel, *American Ceramics* 8, no. 2 (1990): 47.

15 Paul Mathieu quoted in Bruce Hugh Russell, "Suite Serpentin," in *The Pottery of Mathieu: Suite Serpentin* (Ontario, Canada: Burlington Art Center; Calgary, Alberta, Canada: Stride Gallery, 1998), 4.

16 Bruce Hugh Russell, "Suite Serpentin," 4.

17 See Elaine Levin, *Ceramics Monthly* 42, no. 10 (December 1994): 49–53.

18 Guggenheim Museum, *The Italian Metamorphosis, 1943–1968* (New York: Harry N. Abrams, 1994), 709.

19 Christopher Knight, *Andrew Lord* (New York: Blum Helman Gallery, 1986), unpag.

20 Paul Rice and Christopher Gowing, *British Studio Ceramics* (London: Barrie and Jenkins, 1989), 186.

21 Craig Owens, "The Allegorical Impulse: Toward a Theory of Postmodernism," *October,* no. 12 (spring 1980): 69.

22 Walter Benjamin, *The Origins of Greek Tragic Drama,* trans. John Osborne (London: New Left Books, 1977), 178.

23 Virgilio Vercelloni, *European Gardens: An Historical Atlas* (New York: Rizzoli, 1990), 54.

24 Conversation with Adrian Saxe, 27 August 1999.

25 Ibid.

26 Conversation with Liza Lou, 26 August 1999.

Tom Rippon, United States, b. 1954.
Teacup on a Column, 1984. Porcelain,
lusters, pencil, acrylic. W.: 8 in. Gift
of the Estate of Betty M. Asher.
TR.12800.225.12.

Ralph Bacerra, United States, b. 1938.
Drum Bowl, 1988. Whiteware. W.: 23 in. Gift
of Howard and Gwen Laurie Smits in honor
of LACMA's twenty-fifth anniversary.
M.90.82.2.

Gwen Laurie Smits

Tribute to a Collector

GRETCHEN ADKINS

My mother, Gwen Laurie Smits, was born with the collecting gene and a keen aesthetic sense. In college she took art history and loved it, and as a young mother (before the current extensive commercial marketing of art), she pasted postcards of the paintings of Vincent van Gogh in a scrapbook. She wanted a record of everything he had ever painted. She told me stories of severed ears and yellow chairs, and she made me feel a vicarious thrill when van Gogh left rainy Paris and found intense sun in Arles. When his catalogue raisonné was published, she lost interest in the postcard project and wanted to collect the real thing. Van Goghs were out of the question, but she began to test her critical eye in the nascent Los Angeles art scene of the 1960s. Still, the exercise was not satisfying, because she had to save too long between purchases, and her resources did not allow her to obtain the best work of the artists she most admired.

Her breakthrough came with pots, the collection she and my father, Howard Smits, eventually gave to the Los Angeles County Museum of Art. She didn't recognize her pots as an art collection until 1979, but she'd been buying them for years. Throughout my childhood, we always had bouquets of fresh flowers in the house, on which Mother lavished time and energy. She grew flowers to match the decor of the house, and she varied the containers as often as the arrangements, squirreling away quarters from the household budget to buy yet another vase. She didn't think of her vases as an extravagance

Opposite:
Hans Coper, Germany, active England, 1920–1981. *Spade-Shaped Vase,* c. 1969. Stoneware. H.: 11½ in. Gift of Howard and Gwen Laurie Smits. M.87.1.27.

because she used them. The closet off the lanai housed eighty containers, each one lovingly chosen for its shape, color, or size. Some were suitable for Ikebana, the Japanese art of flower arrangement, which she had studied. Others complemented the greens of the living room. The favorites were outfitted with frogs secured with florist's clay so they would be ready at a moment's need. She purchased a crater-glazed bowl by Otto and Gertrud Natzler because she had never seen such a refined yet rough texture, and a footed bowl by Harrison McIntosh because she loved the restrained surface decoration. The vases kept coming, but she didn't consider them a collection.

Howard and Gwen Laurie Smits in front of a selection of their collection of contemporary ceramics, in their house in San Marino, California, 1984. Photograph by Grey Crawford.

And then one day she bought a pot that couldn't be used. After raising her daughters, she traveled as often as she could, usually to see art around the world. In 1969 she was in Amsterdam with the Fellows of Contemporary Art, a philanthropic group of contemporary art enthusiasts who had supported the Pasadena Art Museum until Norton Simon purchased it. After that, the group supported individual artists, mounted exhibitions, and offered its members specialized trips focusing on contemporary art. The Fellows had visited the collections of the Stedelijk Museum and were on their way to a reception in the director's office, when Mom saw an object on display unlike any she had seen before. "Where can I buy a piece like that?" she asked. "There's a gallery down the street," the curator responded. So instead of attending the reception, my mother headed out of the museum, turned left, and bought a twelve-inch *Spade-Shaped Vase* (p. 240) by Hans Coper for $103. The spade is one of Coper's classic shapes, a flattened, thrown bowl, pinched on the bottom and supported by a column that thrusts into the rectangular pouch. On this piece, shadows hover at the junction of base and bowl, emphasizing the sense of invasion by the lighter-hued stem. The vessel makes a dynamic statement of contrasts: post/lintel, erect/soft, light/dark, masculine/feminine. Incised gossamer lines give texture to the stoneware and act as threads binding the form. Coper's work is one of the icons of twentieth-century ceramics, and this piece presents the artist at his best.

On my next visit home, Mom proudly showed me this purchase, stroking its surface as she spoke of her adventure. She'd had no idea who Hans Coper was and assumed he was Dutch because she had bought his work in Holland. All she knew was that she loved the deceptive simplicity of the form and the subtle markings on the surface. She asked guiltily, "Do you think it's an indulgence to buy a vase you can't put flowers in?" (In fact, Coper has said that all of his pots could hold flowers, but perhaps she was uneasy adding any element that would mar the sculptural form of *Spade-Shaped Vase.*)

Martin Smith, England, b. 1950.

Above, left:
Bowl, c. 1979. Red earthenware glazed with epoxy. W.: 13 in. Gift of Howard and Gwen Laurie Smits. M.87.1.157.

Above, right:
Two Angular Forms, 1979. Earthenware. W.: 20½ in. Gift of Howard and Gwen Laurie Smits. M.87.1.156a-b.

In the spring of 1979, Mother returned from a trip to England with two Lucie Rie pots (p. 102, bottom left, and p. 103) she had bought in Bath and a deconstructed vessel by the then-unknown Martin Smith from Liberty's of London (above left). She was sharing her purchases with Dad when he recognized the impassioned urgency in her voice. This was a woman with a conviction. "Why not collect pots instead of paintings?" he said. "We'll set aside $100 a month." He was content to let her make the artistic decisions, since he had always been more of a patron of his wife than of the arts. It was one of the nicest presents my father ever gave my mother. From then on she eschewed paintings and started to openly admit she was a collector of ceramics.

At the time, she didn't know anyone who collected ceramics, and so she had no role model. She had visited many private art collections with the Fellows, but they were of paintings and sculpture. No established gallery system existed to promote contemporary ceramics. But then, in that same year, the groundbreaking exhibition *A Century of Ceramics,* curated by Garth Clark and Margie Hughto, opened at the Everson Museum in Syracuse. Mom flew across the country to see it. A whole museum exhibition devoted to contemporary ceramics! It was a watershed in her life. She bought the catalogue and read and reread it, underlining and highlighting until the binding gave way and the pages fell out. Then she bought another copy. She was on her way to learning about American ceramics.

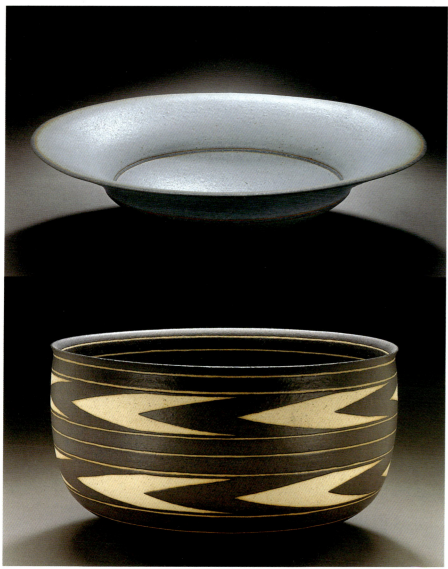

Alev Ebüzziya Siesbye, Turkey, b. 1938.

Top:
Large Platter, 1983. Stoneware. Diam.: 21 in. Gift of Howard and Gwen Laurie Smits. M.87.1.152.

Above:
Black-and-White Bowl, 1983. Stoneware, hand-coiled and oxidization fired, with wax-resist decoration. Diam.: 13 in. Gift of Howard and Gwen Laurie Smits. M.87.1.153.

Mom's timing was felicitous. Adventuresome dealers began to showcase ceramics at galleries such as Alice Westfall's Exhibit A in Chicago, Ken Deaver's American Hand in Washington, D.C., Theo Portnoy in New York, Helen Drutt in Philadelphia, and Jo Ann Raap's The Hand and the Spirit in Scottsdale, Arizona. Soon Garth Clark and Mark del Vecchio opened a gallery committed exclusively to ceramic vessels on Wilshire Boulevard, across the street from LACMA. "Garth gave me confidence about ceramics...that it was O.K. to collect them," she recalls. "Here was a dealer who was focusing on what I loved best!" She went to nearly every exhibition the gallery organized.

Collecting is a demanding taskmaster, if given free rein. It drives the daily schedule. It dominates the thought. And it dictates how money is spent. Mother had a hard time keeping within the pot allowance. She started to devise ways for her budget-respectful soul to allow her ceramics-besotted heart to have its way. She saw a show of Alev Siesbye's coil-built vessels, and it was love at first sight. The matte surfaces on elegant forms and restrained decoration were right up Mom's alley. She coveted two pieces in particular. One was a low, open bowl, swelling up from an all-but-invisible foot, with a double

welt of unglazed clay midway both inside and out. The other was as bold in design as Siesbye ever gets, with two dominating bands of beige chevrons racing around the girth of the charcoal bowl. She loved them both but could afford only one for the collection. Fortunately, she and Dad were about to celebrate their fiftieth wedding anniversary, traditionally celebrated with presents of gold, but stoneware was more to Mom's taste. Over cocktails she broached the question of how they should honor the longevity of their marriage, and by the time dinner was served she had convinced my father that they should give each other a Siesbye. So Mother bought the blue vessel, and they gave each other the charcoal one. I asked Dad how he felt about receiving a ceramic for his golden anniversary. He shrugged: "Whatever makes your mother happy." Both vessels are now in the museum's collection.

Once Mom accepted the mandate of collecting pots, she no longer felt the need to use them. She could view them as art, and their beauty was reason enough to own them. She began to refer to the collection as though it were a living being with its own appetite and demands, and she believed it was her job to meet its needs. Occasionally she purchased a piece of ceramic sculpture that she coveted, such as *Jackson Pollock,* 1983, by Robert Arneson (p. 158), which combined her interest in contemporary painting with her innate love of clay, but the collection remained one primarily of vessels.

When Mom was offered the six-foot sculpture *Lady with Hat* by Viola Frey, her respect for separate budgets was badly threatened. She loved the piece, but how to afford it? Should she spend the food money? The clothing allowance? At last she decided on debt, but creative debt. She suggested that the ceramic grandmother figure should be her birthday present from Dad for the next five years. Each year on March 9 she announced that she now "owned" another fifth. This is one piece she could not bring herself to give away when in 1987 she and Dad decided to donate the collection.

There were several reasons for the decision to donate. Earthquakes are a constant potential threat in Southern California, and Mom and Dad knew that they could not ensure the safety of the collection. Also, they were moving to smaller quarters, where there wouldn't be room to live with the collection, and they agreed that it made no sense to box and store it. They wanted the collection to be a resource for students of all ages at an institution in the community they had known all of their adult lives.

They invited LACMA to take whatever it wished. That initial selection and their subsequent gifts amount to more than three hundred pieces. Since then, Jo Lauria, assistant curator of decorative arts, has increased the scope of the collection by purchasing key pieces of large sculpture. With her enthusiastic energy, the Smits collection is stronger then ever.

I asked Mom recently if there are any pieces that she particularly misses. She answered without hesitation: "*Suspicious Wife Plate* by Beatrice Wood (p. 245). I saw it in Garth's office on Wilshire and I had to have it. And I'm sorry I don't have it now." The plate, from 1952, early in Wood's ceramics career, bears her characteristic lighthearted, spare drawing. The figure's eyes have a yin-yang relationship, the badly cut hair is impossibly straight, and the overall style is similar to the work of Paul Klee.

The short decade when Mom was an active collector of pots was one of the happiest in her life. She felt a sense of accomplishment and gained recognition within a world she had always loved. And rather than looking on the donation as a loss, she realizes that more people will be able to enjoy the objects she cherishes at LACMA, particularly when they travel to new venues in exhibitions such as this one.

Gretchen Adkins is associate director of the Garth Clark Gallery in New York. She earned her MA in art history in 1987 and has published articles in *American Ceramics, American Craft, Ceramics Art and Perception,* and *Kerameiki Techni.* As a member of the board of directors of the Katonah Museum of Art, she curated a number of exhibitions, including *Islamic Images* and *Three Dimensions: Glass, Clay, Fiber.*

Selected Bibliography

Adlin, Jane, ed. *Contemporary Ceramics: Selections from the Metropolitan Museum of Art.* Exh. cat. New York: Metropolitan Museum of Art, 1998.

Anfam, David. *Abstract Expressionism.* London: Thames and Hudson, 1990.

Art Alliance, California State University, Fullerton, ed. *Contemporary Ceramics: The Artists of TB-9.* Text by Elaine Levin. Exh. cat. Fullerton, Calif.: Main Art Gallery, California State University, 1989.

Benezra, Neal. *Robert Arneson: A Retrospective.* Exh. cat. Des Moines: Des Moines Art Center, 1985.

Berensohn, Paulus. *Finding One's Way with Clay.* Dallas: Biscuit Books, 1972.

Berns, Marla C. *Ceramic Gestures: New Vessels by Magdalene Odundo.* Exh. cat. Santa Barbara, Calif.: University Art Museum, University of California, 1995.

Binns, Charles F. *The Potter's Craft.* 1910. Reprint, New York: D. Van Nostrand Co., 1947.

Birks, Tony. *The Complete Potter's Companion.* Boston: Little, Brown, 1993.

Bismanis, Maija, ed. *Marilyn Levine: A Retrospective.* Essay by Timothy Long. Exh. cat. Saskatchewan, Canada: MacKenzie Art Gallery, 1998.

Bray, Hazel. *The Potter's Art in California, 1885–1955.* Exh. cat. Oakland, Calif.: Oakland Museum, 1980.

Cardew, Michael. *Pioneer Pottery.* Exh. cat. New York: St. Martin's, 1969.

Carney, Margaret, ed. *Alfred Teaches Ceramics, 1900–1996.* Exh. cat. Alfred, N.Y.: Museum of Ceramic Art at Alfred, 1996.

———. *What You Give You Keep Forever: The Vivika and Otto Heino Retrospective.* Essays by Margaret Carney, Val Cushing, and Gerry Williams. Exh. cat. Alfred, N.Y.: Museum of Ceramic Art at Alfred, 1995.

Castile, Rand. *The Way of Tea.* New York: Weatherhill, 1971.

Clark, Garth. *American Ceramics: 1876 to the Present.* New York: Abbeville, 1990.

———. *American Potters: The Work of Twenty Modern Masters.* New York: Watson-Guptill, 1981.

———. *The Book of Cups.* New York: Abbeville, 1990.

———. *Ceramic Echoes: Historical References in Contemporary Ceramics.* Exh. cat. Kansas City, Mo.: Nelson-Atkins Museum of Art, 1983.

———. *The Eccentric Teapot: Four Hundred Years of Invention.* New York: Abbeville, 1989.

———. *The Potter's Art: A Complete History of Pottery in Britain.* London: Phaidon Press, 1995.

Clark, Garth, ed. *Ceramic Art: Comment and Review, 1882–1977.* New York: E. P. Dutton, 1978.

Clark, Garth, and Margie Hughto (preface). *A Century of Ceramics in the United States, 1878–1978.* Exh. cat. New York: E. P. Dutton in association with Everson Museum of Art, 1979.

Coatts, Margot, ed. *Pioneers of Modern Craft.* Manchester: Manchester University Press, 1997.

Conrads, David, and Deni McIntosh McHenry, eds. *Ken Ferguson.* Exh. cat. Kansas City: Nelson-Atkins Museum of Art, 1995.

Coplans, John. *Abstract Expressionist Ceramics.* Exh. cat. Irvine, Calif.: Art Gallery, University of California, 1966.

Craft and Folk Art Museum, Los Angeles, ed. *Natzler: The Ceramics of Gertrud and Otto Natzler (1971–1977).* Exh. cat. Los Angeles: Craft and Folk Art Museum, 1977.

Crafts Advisory Committee, ed. *Michael Cardew.* Introduction by Bernard Leach. Contributions by Michael Cardew, Ray Finch, John Houston, and Katherine Pleydell Bouverie. Exh. cat. New York: Watson-Guptill, 1976.

Creative Arts League of San Francisco, ed. *Viola Frey: Retrospective.* Essay by Garth Clark. Exh. cat. Oakland, Calif.: Crocker Art Museum, 1981.

De Waal, Edmund. *Bernard Leach.* London: Tate Gallery Publishing, 1998.

Dormer, Peter, ed. *The Culture of Craft.* Manchester: Manchester University Press, 1997.

———. *The New Ceramics: Trends and Traditions.* London: Thames and Hudson, 1986.

Dreisbach, Janice T., ed. *Robert Brady: A Survey Exhibition.* Essays by Thomas H. Garver and John Fitz Gibbon. Exh. cat. Sacramento, Calif.: Crocker Art Museum, 1989.

Failing, Patricia. *Howard Kottler: Face to Face.* Seattle and London: University of Washington Press, 1995.

Fineberg, Jonathan. *Art Since 1940: Strategies of Being.* New York: Harry N. Abrams, 1995.

———. *War Heads and Others: Robert Arneson.* Exh. cat. New York: Allan Frumkin Gallery, 1983.

Foley, Suzanne. *A Decade of Ceramic Art, 1962–1972.* Exh. cat. San Francisco: San Francisco Museum of Art, 1972.

Fuller Goldeen Gallery, ed. *Robert Arneson.* Text by Donald Kuspit. Exh. cat. San Francisco: Fuller Goldeen Gallery; 1985.

Garrels, Gary, and Janet Bishop, eds. *Robert Arneson: Self-Reflections.* Essay by Jonathan Fineberg. Exh. cat. San Francisco: San Francisco Museum of Art, 1997.

Goodrich, Lloyd. *Art of the United States, 1670–1966.* Exh. cat. New York: Whitney Museum of American Art, 1966.

Graham, Patricia. *Tea of the Sages: The Art of Sencha.* Honolulu: University of Hawaii Press, 1998.

Halper, Vicki. *Clay Revisions: Plate, Cup, Vase.* Exh. cat. Seattle: Seattle Art Museum, 1987.

Halper, Vicki, ed. *Strong Tea: Richard Notkin and the Yixing Tradition.* Exh. cat. Seattle: Seattle Art Museum, 1990.

Hamada, Shōji. *The Retrospective Exhibition of Shōji Hamada.* Exh. cat. Tokyo: National Museum of Modern Art, 1977.

Harris, Mary Emma. *The Arts at Black Mountain College.* Cambridge, Mass.: MIT Press, 1987.

Haskell, Barbara, ed. *John Mason Ceramic Sculpture.* Exh. cat. Pasadena, Calif.: Pasadena Museum of Modern Art, 1974.

Haulk, Tom. *American Clay II.* Exh. cat. Baltimore: Meredith Contemporary Art, 1982.

Herman, Lloyd E., ed. *Form and Fire: Natzler Ceramics 1939–1972.* Exh. cat. Washington, D.C.: Smithsonian Institution Press, 1973.

Hodin, J. P. *Bernard Leach: A Potter's Work.* London: Jupiter Books, 1977.

Hogben, Carol, ed. *The Art of Bernard Leach.* New York: Watson-Guptill, 1978.

Hudson River Museum, ed. *John Mason: Installations from the Hudson River Series.* Essays by Catherine Conn and Rosalind Krauss. Exh. cat. Yonkers, N.Y.: Hudson River Museum, 1978.

Hughto, Margie. *New Works in Clay by Contemporary Painters and Sculptors.* Exh. cat. Syracuse, N.Y.: Everson Museum of Art, 1976.

Humbler, Douglas, with Kay Koeninger, Mary Longtin, and Max van Balgooy. *Earth and Fire: The Marer Collection of Contemporary Ceramics.* Exh. cat. Claremont, Calif.: Galleries of the Claremont Colleges, 1984.

Institute of Contemporary Art, Boston, ed. *Marilyn Levine: A Decade of Ceramic Sculpture.* Essay by Stephen Prokopoff. Exh. cat. Boston: Institute of Contemporary Art, 1981.

John Natsoulas Gallery, ed. *30 Years of TB-9: A Tribute to Robert Arneson.* Exh. cat. Davis, Calif.: John Natsoulas Gallery, 1991.

John Natsoulas Press, ed. *David Gilhooly.* Davis, Calif.: John Natsoulas Press, 1992.

Kardon, Janet. *Gertrud and Otto Natzler: Collaboration/ Solitude.* Exh. cat. New York: American Craft Museum, 1993.

Kuspit, Donald. *Stephen De Staebler: The Figure.* Exh. cat. San Francisco: Chronicle Books in collaboration with Laguna Art Museum and Saddleback College, [1987].

Lang Gallery, Scripps College, ed. *A Retrospective: In Honor of Paul Soldner, Professor of Art, Scripps College.* Essays by Elaine Levin, Mac McClain, and Mary Davis MacNaughton. Exh. cat. Claremont, Calif.: Scripps College; Seattle and London: University of Washington Press, 1991.

Larsen, Susan C. *Viola Frey: Monumental Figures 1978–1987.* Exh. cat. Los Angeles: Asher-Faure; San Francisco: Rena Bransten Gallery, 1988.

Leach, Bernard. *Beyond East and West: Memoirs, Portraits, and Essays.* New York: Watson-Guptill, 1978.

————. *A Potter's Book.* London: Faber and Faber, 1940.

————. *The Potter's Challenge.* Ed. David Outerbridge. New York: E.P. Dutton, 1975.

Lebow, Edward, ed. *The Ceramics of Ken Price.* Exh. cat. Houston: Menil Collection, Houston Fine Art Press, 1992.

Levin, Elaine. *Glen Lukens: Pioneer of the Vessel Aesthetic.* Exh. cat. Los Angeles: Fine Arts Gallery, California State University, 1982.

————. *The History of American Ceramics from 1607 to the Present: From Pipkins and Bean Pots to Contemporary Forms.* New York: Harry N. Abrams, 1988.

————. *Illusionistic-Realism Defined in Contemporary Ceramic Sculpture.* Exh. cat. Laguna Beach, Calif.: Laguna Beach Museum of Art, 1977.

————. *Ten Years Later: Ed Blackburn, Tony Costanzo, Robert Rasmussen (a.k.a. Redd Ekks), John Roloff, Richard Shaw.* Exh. cat. Fullerton, Calif.: Main Art Gallery, Visual Arts Center, California State University, 1987.

Lippard, Lucy, ed. *Overlay: Contemporary Art and the Art of Prehistory.* New York: Pantheon Books, 1983.

Lord, Andrew. *Andrew Lord: New Work.* Text by Christopher Knight. Exh. cat. New York: Blum Helman Gallery, 1986.

Los Angeles County Museum of Art. *The Ceramic Work of Gertrud and Otto Natzler: A Retrospective Exhibition.* Exh. cat. Los Angeles: Los Angeles County Museum of Art, 1966.

————. *Gertrud and Otto Natzler Ceramics.* Exh. cat. Los Angeles: Los Angeles County Museum of Art, 1968.

————. *John Mason: Sculpture.* Introduction by John Coplans. Exh. cat. Los Angeles: Los Angeles County Museum of Art, 1966.

————. *Ken Price: Happy's Curios.* Essay by Maurice Tuchman. Exh. cat. Los Angeles: Los Angeles County Museum of Art, 1935.

————. *Peter Voulkos: Sculpture.* Exh. cat. Los Angeles: Los Angeles County Museum of Art, 1965.

————. *Robert Irwin/Kenneth Price.* Essay by Lucy Lippard. Exh. cat. Los Angeles: Los Angeles County Museum of Art, 1966.

Lucero, Michael. *Sculpture 1976–1995.* Exh. cat. New York: Hudson Hills Press in association with Mint Museum of Art, Charlotte, N.C., 1996.

Lynn, Martha Drexler. *The Clay Art of Adrian Saxe.* Los Angeles: Los Angeles County Museum of Art; New York and London: Thames and Hudson, 1993.

————. *Clay Today: Contemporary Ceramists and Their Work: A Catalogue of the Howard and Gwen Laurie Smits Collection at the Los Angeles County Museum of Art.* Los Angeles: Los Angeles County Museum of Art; San Francisco: Chronicle Books, 1990.

McCready, Karen. *Contemporary American Ceramics: Twenty Artists.* Exh. cat. Newport Beach, Calif.: Newport Harbor Art Museum, 1985.

Mackenzie, Warren, and Valerie Tvrdik. *Minnesota Pottery: A Potter's View.* Exh. cat. Minneapolis, Minn.: University Gallery, 1981.

MacNaughton, Mary Davis. *Revolution in Clay: The Marer Collection of Contemporary Ceramics.* Exh. cat. Essays by Kay Koeninger, Mary Davis MacNaughton, and Martha Drexler Lynn. Claremont, Calif.: Ruth Chandler Williamson Gallery, Scripps College; Seattle and Washington: University of Washington Press, 1994.

Manhart, Tom, and Marcia Manhart, eds. *The Eloquent Object: The Evolution of American Art in Craft Media since 1945.* Exh. cat. Tulsa, Okla.: Philbrook Museum of Art; Seattle: University of Washington Press, 1987.

Marshall, Richard, and Suzanne Foley. *Ceramic Sculpture: Six Artists.* Exh. cat. New York: Whitney Museum of American Art, 1981.

Massaro, Karen Thuesen. *Time and Place: Fifty Years of Santa Cruz Studio Ceramics.* Exh. cat. Santa Cruz, Calif.: Museum of Art and History, Santa Cruz, 1997.

Mattl-Wurm, Sylvia. *Natzler Keramiken, 1935–1990.* Exh. cat. Vienna: Judischen und des Historischen Museums der Stadt Wien in collaboration with American Craft Museum, New York, 1994.

Mills College Art Gallery, ed. *Ron Nagle: A Survey Exhibition.* Essay by Michael McTwigan. Exh. cat. Oakland, Calif.: Mills College Art Gallery, 1993.

Mingeikan/USA Tour, ed. *Mingei: Two Centuries of Japanese Folk Art.* Exh. cat. Tokyo: International Programs Department, Japan Folk Crafts Museum, 1995.

Munsterberg, Hugo, and Marjorie Munsterberg. *World Ceramics: From Prehistoric to Modern Times.* New York: Penguin, 1998.

Museum Boijmans Van Beuningen, ed. *Geert Lap: The Thrown Form.* Exh. cat. Rotterdam: Museum Boijmans Van Beuningen, 1988.

————. *Martin Smith: Balance and Space, Ceramics 1976–1996.* Contributions by Dorris U. Kuyken-Schneider, Martin Smith, Alison Britton, and Margreet Eijkelenboom-Vermeer. Exh. cat. Rotterdam: Museum Boijmans Van Beuningen, 1996.

Museum of Applied Arts, Helsinki, ed. *Rudolf Staffel: Searching for Light.* Essays by Marianne Aav and Rudolf Staffel. Exh. cat. Helsinki: Museum of Applied Arts in collaboration with Philadelphia Museum of Art, 1996.

National Museum of Modern Art, Kyoto, ed. *Toshiko Takaezu: Retrospective.* Essay by Ruiko Kato. Exh. Cat. Kyoto: National Museum of Modern Art, 1995.

Natzler, Otto. *The Ceramic Work of Gertrud and Otto Natzler.* Exh. cat. San Francisco, Calif.: M. H. deYoung Memorial Museum, 1971.

Naumann, Francis M., ed. *Beatrice Wood: A Centennial Tribute.* Exh. cat. New York: American Craft Museum, 1997.

Nordness, Lee. *Objects: USA.* Exh. cat. New York: Viking, 1970.

Octagon Center for the Arts, ed. *British Ceramics Today.* Exh. cat. [Ames, Iowa]: Octagon Center for the Arts, 1980.

Olympic Arts Festival, ed. *Art in Clay: 1950s to 1980s in Southern California.* Exh. cat. Contributions by Betty Sheinbaum, Susan Peterson, Gerald Nordlund, and Eudorah M. Moore. Los Angeles: Los Angeles Municipal Art Gallery, 1984.

Perry, Barbara A., ed. *American Ceramics: The Collection of Everson Museum of Art.* New York: Rizzoli, 1989.

Peterson, Susan. *The Craft and Art of Clay.* Woodstock, N.Y.: Overlook, 1996.

————. *Shōji Hamada: A Potter's Way and Work.* New York and Tokyo: Weatherhill, 1995.

Piet Stockmans. Exh. cat. Tielt, Lannoo, The Netherlands: Cultural Ambassador of Flanders, 1996.

Poor, Henry Varnum. *A Book of Pottery: From Mud to Immortality.* Englewood Cliffs, N.J.: Prentice-Hall, 1958.

Press, Nancy Neumann, ed. *Marguerite: A Retrospective Exhibition of the Work of Master Potter Marguerite Wildenhain.* Exh. cat. Ithaca, N.Y.: Herbert F. Johnson Museum of Art, Cornell University, 1980.

Pucker Gallery, Boston. *Brother Thomas: Gifts from the Fire II.* Exh. cat. Boston: Pucker Gallery, 1995.

————. *Gifts from the Fire: The Porcelains of Brother Thomas.* Exh. cat. Boston: Pucker Gallery, 1993.

The Quiet Eye: Pottery of Shōji Hamada and Bernard Leach. Essays by Susan Peterson and Warren Mackenzie. Exh. cat. Monterey, Calif.: Monterey Peninsula Museum of Art in collaboration with San Francisco Craft and Folk Art Museum, 1990.

Ramsey, John. *American Potters and Pottery.* New York: Tudor Publishing, 1947.

Rice, Paul, and Christopher Gowing (appendices). *British Studio Ceramics in the 20th Century.* Radnor, Pa.: Chilton Book Company, 1989.

Richards, Mary Caroline. *Centering: In Pottery, Poetry, and the Person.* Middletown, Conn.: Wesleyan University Press, 1964.

Rigden, Timothy. *American Studio Ceramics, 1920–1950.* Exh. cat. Minneapolis: University Art Museum, University of Minnesota, Minneapolis, 1988.

Rudy Autio. Exh. cat. [Missoula, Mont.]:University of Montana, 1983.

Sanders, Herbert H., and Kenkichi Tomimoto. *The World of Japanese Ceramics: Historical and Modern Techniques.* Tokyo: Kodansha International, 1976.

Schlanger, Jeff, and Toshiko Takaezu. *Maija Grotell: Works Which Grow from Belief.* Exh. cat. Goffstown, N.H.: Studio Potter Books, 1996.

Schwartz, Marvin, and Richard Wolfe. *A History of American Art Porcelain.* New York: Renaissance Editions, 1967.

Selz, Peter. *Funk.* Exh. cat. Berkeley, Calif.: University Art Museum, 1967.

Selz, Peter, ed. *Harold Paris: The California Years.* Exh. cat. Berkeley, Calif.: University Art Museum, 1972.

Sewell, Darrel, ed. *Philadelphia: Three Centuries of American Art.* Philadelphia: Philadelphia Museum of Art, 1976.

Sezon Museum of Art, ed. *Peter Voulkos: Retrospective.* Essay by Rose Slivka. Exh. cat. Tokyo: Sezon Museum of Art; Kyoto: National Museum of Modern Art, 1995.

Slivka, Rose, ed. *West Coast Ceramics.* Exh. Cat. Amsterdam: Stedelijk Museum, 1979.

Slivka, Rose, and Karen Tsujimoto. *The Art of Peter Voulkos.* Exh. cat. Tokyo: Kodansha International in collaboration with Oakland Museum, 1995.

Stedelijk Museum, Amsterdam, ed. *Keramik in Het Stedelijk.* Amsterdam: Stedelijk Museum, 1998.

Tempest in a Teapot: The Ceramic Art of Peter Shire. Texts by Hunter Drohojowska, Norman H. Klein, and Ettore Sottsass. New York: Rizzoli, 1991.

Tunis, Roslyn. *Ancient Inspirations, Contemporary Interpretations.* Exh. cat. Binghamton, N.Y.: Robertson Center for the Arts and Sciences, 1982.

Visual Arts Center, California State University, Fullerton, ed. *Beatrice Wood: Retrospective.* Essays by Francis M. Naumann and Garth Clark. Exh. cat. Fullerton, Calif.: Main Gallery, Visual Arts Center California State University, 1983.

Watson, Oliver. *Studio Pottery: Twentieth Century British Ceramics in the Victoria and Albert Museum.* London: Phaidon Press in association with Victoria and Albert Museum, 1993.

Wechsler, Susan. *Low-Fire Ceramics: A New Direction in American Clay.* New York: Watson-Guptill, 1981.

Whybrow, Marion. *St Ives, 1883–1993: Portrait of an Art Colony.* Introduction by David Brown. Woodbridge, England: Antique Collectors' Club, 1994, reprinted 1996.

Wildenhain, Marguerite. *The Invisible Core: A Potter's Life and Thoughts.* Palo Alto, Calif.: Pacific Books, 1973.

————. *Pottery: Form and Expression.* New York: American Craftsmen's Council, 1959.

Wilson, Janet. *Skilled Work: American Craft in the Renwick Gallery.* Exh. cat. Washington, D.C.: Smithsonian Institution Press, 1998.

Wood, Beatrice. *I Shock Myself: The Autobiography of Beatrice Wood.* Ed. Lindsay Smith. San Francisco: Chronicle Books, 1985.

Yanagi, Sōetsu. *The Unknown Craftsman: A Japanese Insight into Beauty.* Tokyo: Kodansha International, 1982.

Index

Tea Cups 1989 Chris Curtis

Tea Cups 1989 Chris Cart